ROAD DOG

ROAD DOG

LIFE AND REFLECTIONS FROM THE ROAD AS A STAND-UP COMIC

DOV DAVIDOFF

ST. MARTIN'S PRESS ✹ NEW YORK

ROAD DOG. Copyright © 2017 by Dov Davidoff. All rights reserved. Printed in the United States of America. For information, address St. Martin's Press, 175 Fifth Avenue, New York, N.Y. 10010.

www.stmartins.com

Designed by Steven Seighman

The Library of Congress Cataloging-in-Publication Data

Names: Davidoff, Dov author.
Title: Road dog : life and reflections from the road as a stand-up comic / Dov Davidoff.
Description: First edition. | New York : St. Martin's, 2017.
Identifiers: LCCN 2017021360| ISBN 978-1-250-03807-4 (hardcover) | ISBN 978-1-250-03806-7 (ebook)
Subjects: LCSH: Davidoff, Dov. | Comedians—United States— Biography.
Classification: LCC PN2287.D313 A3 2017 | DDC 792.7/6028092 [B] —dc23
LC record available at https://lccn.loc.gov/2017021360

Our books may be purchased in bulk for promotional, educational, or business use. Please contact your local bookseller or the Macmillan Corporate and Premium Sales Department at 1-800-221-7945, extension 5442, or by email at MacmillanSpecialMarkets@macmillan.com.

First Edition: October 2017

10   9   8   7   6   5   4   3   2   1

This book is dedicated to my wife, who encourages me and shows me love. Her incessant nagging to finish this book is part of why it now exists. You've helped me to care less about what I think and more about how I feel; for that I am indebted to you; also for other stuff, but if I were prioritizing, that would be even higher than doing laundry and stuffing bits of steel wool into the stove to prevent mice from entering the house. All jokes aside, I love you very much.

It's also dedicated to people all over this country, and in a few other parts of the world, who went out of their way to buy a ticket and make it to some club to sit in some dark room with a PA system and listen to what I had to say. I hope you were entertained. I take your time very seriously. I really appreciate you.

And to the hecklers—what can I say? I hope you find the self-love you need to prevent you from crying out for no apparent reason in a room full of decent people, and stepping on my punch lines; until then, go fuck yourselves.

ACKNOWLEDGMENTS

I would like to thank my friend Sam Sheridan, who inadvertently is also the most impressive human being I know. Thanks for encouraging me to write this, and introducing me to your, and now my, agent, David Kuhn. After reading this book Sam may regret doing both. I'd like to thank David for pushing to find a publisher for this book. It wasn't easy. I'd like to thank my mother for endowing me with a reflective capacity, and reinforcing that capacity by raising me in such a way that for the rest of my life I'd likely have to spend some aspect of myself untying the strange knots of my childhood. To the Comedy Cellar (Estee, Ava, Noam): thank you for everything, but especially for providing me with a comedic home. You have no idea how meaningful that has been to me. To the Monday-night dinners with Andy, Dan, and Sandy: I can't thank you in an earnest way, as I'd be eaten alive for having expressed any vulnerability, but suffice it to say you've made Monday evenings something worth looking forward to—no small thing. I'd like to thank Anthony Tambakis; your encouragement meant much to me. I'd also like to thank Dom Irrera for his friendship, and for telling me that story about having found a slice of pizza in his pocket while playing Ping-Pong. To my agent, Justin Edbrooke, thank you for your professionalism and your support. Thank you to Jamie Masada, whose memory never ceases to bring a smile to my face. I miss you. A thank-you to my brother Orion for being there for me when I came back to New York from LA, a particularly low point in my life. I'd like to thank the Tampellinis (Angela, John, Robert, David, and Pete) for making me feel like I have more family than I actually do. And last, but not least, "the one, the only," the "Can Do Kid," the great Bryan Callen; your friendship, warmth, hilarity, and generosity have never wavered. You are loved, mostly by yourself, but also by me, and many many others.

AUTHOR'S NOTE

This is a true story, though some names and details have been changed.

PREFACE

Where to begin . . . I'm not a real writer. I'm a bit dyslexic. Daylight saving time still confuses me, and I have a short attention span. I can't stand sitting for long periods of time. I was thrown out of high school for behavioral issues and will likely spend the rest of my life proving that I'm better than the chaotic situation I come from, even though I will never actually feel that way inside. And yet, I've always wanted to write a book. Why? Who knows? To prove to myself that I can? To discover the truth or get closer to it, whatever that means. To search. Dig. Find. Think. Question. Ponder. Feel. Here goes . . .

ALSO . . . this is not a collection of essays, but the chapters will not always follow one another in terms of narrative; that's just the way it came out of me. However, by the end, there will be a kind of continuity—

a "dovetailing," so to speak. I will bring things back around in such a way that you will hopefully feel as though a story has been told.

The chapters have been named after the city or state in which the action or the reflection took place.

ROAD DOG

LAS VEGAS
THE DESERT

Fuck. I hate myself. Cigarette butts and mini-bottles from the minibar keep company with cocaine residue on the coffee table. I feel guilty. What am I doing with my life? What is life? I want to embrace it, but I'm not sure what it is, and I don't think I know how. Maybe I've been running from it for so long that I've forgotten what it looks like. Sub-atomically, even dense matter is, for the most part, empty space. I guess that's kind of how I feel right now, like empty space. I'm here, but I'm not, like a ghost made of flesh and blood.

I worked last night, if you can call it work. I'm a comedian. I was headlining a small venue at some hotel casino off the strip. I'd mention the name, but what's the difference? They're all basically the same. Light reflecting off glittering glass walls, like risqué revue dancers in desert sequin tights, issuing promises they can't keep. Magnificent marble floors clashing with the sounds of bells and whistles, echoing from the Superman slots and the pai gow poker machines. Brilliant, dazzling, dizzying columns of light bursting into a billion pieces, seducing gamblers like mosquitoes irresistibly drawn to bug zappers. The most expensive free drinks in the world are "given away" here.

LAST NIGHT AT THE SHOW

"Dov Davidoff!" calls out the Playboy Bunny, introducing me to the audience as she recedes behind the red-velvet curtains. Exiting the hallway, I step out onto the stage, bathed in light that both blinds and illuminates. I think, *What a strange symbol the Playboy Bunny is.* The distant relative of a rodent with large ears and a bow tie has become so synonymous with sexuality that we've all just accepted it for what it is. I don't get it. Was Hugh Hefner sitting around thinking, *You know, women are sexy . . . but I'd really like to fuck a rabbit?*

Reading the audience, I can spot the faces of the people for whom "free" table drinks are now a bitter irony. Their eyes are circled with dark rings but wide open like an owl's. In some cases, they've ended up here, at my show, as a consolation prize for having lost money in the casino. The pit boss said, "Here, have two tickets to a comedy show . . . on us."

"That's all?" asks the loser with the heartbroken expression on the face.

The pit boss cracks a counterfeit smile. "Tell you what . . . you guys like buffets? Here ya go," he says, handing over two more tickets. "On us." He winks, smiling like a reticulated python waving goodbye to a rabbit he'll catch up with tomorrow. In Vegas, "on us" often means you just got fucked.

Like some kind of living history, these faces tell the story of how Las Vegas came to be an American city— one that's built on the backs of losers. Did these people really think they'd walk away winners? How the hell do they think these buildings got so high? Beware of shiny towers in the desert.

Their expressions register their night's reality, like small fish in a big bowl that have just discovered there's no way out. Depending on the beating these guys took, jokes will never be good enough. These guys are the owners of wallets that ran for office against blackjack tables and roulette wheels and lost by a landslide. Stage left, a bachelorette party celebrates the bride-to-be. Their hair-sprayed heads, covered with plastic penis hats, bobble back and forth to the rhythm of rum.

NEXT DAY: WAKING UP

Back in my room, half-dead, one eye barely open, and with the essence and appearance of a pirate, I look to my left. Little tan nipples atop big fake tits peek out from beneath the down comforter on the king-size bed in my hotel room. *Who is this?* I wonder, sifting through the last six hours like a miner unsuccessfully panning for gold.

I have no idea who these tits belong to. Is it my feature act? A feature is the person who precedes the headliner at a comedy show, also known as a "middle." In this case, my feature was an attractive woman, but I don't think she slept here, or did she? Messy bed hair obscures her face. Like a detective trying to identify a body, I look closer . . . similar haircut, I think, but her breasts weren't this big, and she definitely didn't have large angel wings tattooed on her back. Angel-wing tattoos almost always guarantee that the person wearing them will bear little resemblance to the spiritual being they're meant to represent.

I wish this were the first time I'd woken up next to a woman I didn't know, but it's not. Will I ever be able to sustain a real relationship, or at least one that feels real to me, something life-affirming and connected? Am I really this guy? Aren't there better guys to be? I want to be better . . . whatever that means.

Oh, right! I suddenly realize. *It's that wacky hooker from last night. The one who told me that her New Year's*

resolution was to "be more healthy by cutting down on sugar."
Not that it's ever a bad idea to reduce your crystalline
carbohydrate intake, but I just hope it occurs to her that
she may also want to cut down on the whole "having sex
with strangers like me for money" thing first.

I lost my virginity to a prostitute in Mexico when I was
thirteen. It was the first vacation I'd ever been on. My
father brought us to a resort in Cancún, where I spent
a good part of my first afternoon in the hot tub with my
dick pushed up against the powerful jets. Like a large
adolescent barnacle making its home under the bow
of a sedentary boat, I didn't move. Several passersby
commented on the duration of my visits and my commitment to the tub. My fingers were an eagle's talons,
digging into the concrete lip just above the waterline, and
the most powerful jets in the tub were my prey.

"Are you okay in there?" the poolside attendant
called over to me, wondering why, for the last half hour,
I'd been clutching the concrete like a cracked-out house
cat. My response, more physical than verbal, consisted
of a series of grunts, accompanied by the very same
expression worn by a basset hound rut as it attaches
itself to a leg, any leg.

Below are a couple of paragraphs for context:
I was a chubby kid, and I was ashamed of my

body—and of my haircut, and my secondhand clothes, and the dirt driveway in front of my house. The driveway that lay waiting every night, like a panther in the forest, stalking my white sneakers. God knows I tried to keep them clean like the other kids', but the panther was too powerful, especially after the rain came. At the end of my driveway, separated by twenty feet of road, was another driveway, also dirt, that led to the junkyard I grew up in. More on this later, but felt I needed to provide some context. Context is everything. It's the difference between self-defense and homicide. I hope context will prevent you from not caring about what I have to say. I hope it will allow for a less judgmental perspective when I behave in ways that I'm embarrassed by. Context is a bit like a character witness addressing a jury, hoping to create a more compassionate understanding of the accused. Context can be the difference between walking free or doing life.

This is the context in which I clung to those hot tub jets. The ones that made me feel happy. There wasn't much out there that did, so I developed a romantic alliance with a whirlpool.

The night we arrived at the hotel in Cancún, after check-in, my father slid me a couple of twenties. Like most formerly poor, uneducated people who beat the odds, he carried cash. He said, "Take this . . . in case you need it." He loved me but had a funny way of showing it sometimes. One time he told me, "I thought about having your mother killed . . . but I'd never do that because of you and your brother." A pause ensued as he waited for a thank-you or a gesture in acknowledgment of his self-restraint. He was serious. He was funny. He was sad, and he was lonely. I loved him dearly.

BACK AT THE RESORT

Resorts are boring. Even as a kid I'd heard about sex for money in Mexico, and I wanted to make sure it wasn't just a rumor, so I headed for the exit near a taxi stand. I hopped in a beat-up blue Checker cab that looked like an old, rusty, friendly little whale with headlights.

"Take me to the place with the ladies," I said to the driver.

"*Mujeres?*" he said.

With a look, universally understood by men of all stripes, cultures, and creeds, a look that can only be described as *embarrassed, but thirsty*, I said, "Girls. Ladies."

"Ahh, I see!" he said. In the rearview mirror, I saw him flash a toothy grin as he released the clutch, sending us sputtering into the night.

A presumptuous move for a thirteen-year-old, I know, but like all kids who grow up fast, I developed in ways that I shouldn't have. *I shouldn't be here. I probably shouldn't even want to be here.*

The taxi ground to a dusty halt. I paid the driver and exited the little blue whale in front of an old building. Its crooked walls and uneven rooflines would be described as dilapidated by American standards, but it wasn't so bad by Mexican standards. It was the kind of ramshackle operation you've seen in countless films about guys with guns who ride horses and wear hard faces. It was dark. It was foreboding. It was right up my alley.

For me, even at thirteen, pussy had always trumped fear. I'm sure there was an age requirement, but in a place like this, dollars made you any age you needed to be. I stepped through the paint-chipped doors and took a seat at the bar. My anxious but exhilarated legs dangled more than a foot above the greasy floor. There were five people in the room, including me. Two painted ladies of the evening, another gringo patron, and the guy behind the bar, who looked exactly like you'd imagine he would in an establishment whose beverage selection consisted of beer or tequila. I thought about tequila, but I wasn't that daring. Plus it was already a policy of mine to steer clear of anything with a worm in it. I pointed at a beer and placed a couple of bucks on the bar.

A woman in her late thirties, masked in makeup, approached me with a crooked but sultry smile. She sat on the seat next to mine and shot me a wink before slowly placing her hand on the inside of my upper thigh. "I like this place already," said the hot flash running up my leg, FedExing messages to parts of me I could feel but not understand.

"*Hola,*" she said.

I didn't know what that meant, but it didn't matter to me, or her.

"Ab-re-li-na," she said, pointing to herself. My shy smile let her know I wanted to talk, but couldn't. Like clutch ball players, prostitutes perform beautifully in the awkward spaces.

She calmed me. She wasn't very attractive, but she was kind of sweet, and kind of soothing, and I've never been one to let visual details get in the way of what I want. Her eyelash extensions said, *Follow me*, so I did. "Israel," she called over to the mustachioed man with the flinty eyes behind the bar. She mumbled something in Spanish that must have meant "This won't take long." It struck me as strange that his name was Israel. I didn't know you could name a Mexican *Israel*. I thought, *You can be pretty sure you'll never meet a Jew by the name of Mexico.*

Leaving the main building through the rear door, we walked over to one of several seedy little cabanas with bad lighting and cracked windows. Opening the crooked door, she waved me in. She pulled up her short skirt and lay down on the bed, spreading her legs—fast, but not hurried. Practice makes perfect. Removing a condom from her bra without looking, she beckoned me with her eyes. Cigarette burns dotted the off-white sheet like filthy little stars in a filthy universe. Hunger overcame caution as my slow but deliberate steps carried me to her.

For "twenty dollars American," she may have changed the course of my life. After snacking on my virginity, she ran cold water over a hand towel and rubbed it on her vagina. The businesslike efficiency with which she wiped herself left an indelible impression on me. From time to time, I still think about how difficult her life must have been.

2

LAS VEGAS
HEAD THROBBING

My head is throbbing in my bed as I struggle to wake. After last night, probing my memory is like trying to see through dirty glass. Slowly, my shameful behavior begins to reveal itself to the part of me that tried to suppress it in the first place: my consciousness. This is the part of myself that I've always been running from, that we're all running from, when we run. It's the part that says, "I'm unhappy. I don't feel good. I need something more substantial, more life-affirming, even if I'm not sure what *life-affirming* means."

I feel empty, but what do I do?

I guess the only long-term solution is to listen to my conscience, the better part of myself. The part that says, "You must stare into the black space of your emptiness or you will never identify what you are running from."

I, like most people, have two distinct voices in my head. My CONSCIOUSNESS is one. He's a bespectacled Viennese analyst, with eyes contemplatively tilted toward the ceiling. His head rests against the soft leather of his ergonomically appropriate chair. He sits quietly, waiting for me to spill my guts. Like Errol Morris aiming a camera at the subject of a documentary, he gives me just enough silent rope to hang myself with, and I do.

The second part of me we'll call SEX, DRUGS, AND DISTRACTION. (By the way, I'm including alcohol in my definition of drugs. Also, for the purpose of clarity and tone, I have no problem with sex, drugs, or alcohol, unless they become problems. I felt this disclaimer was necessary, lest ye feel judged, for I am not that guy.)

I will now provide a brief conversation between the angel of CONSCIOUSNESS and the devil of SEX, DRUGS, AND DISTRACTION. This is the conversation that played out in my head during the show last night, and many nights before that, and many nights yet to come.

THE CONVERSATION IN MY HEAD WHILE ONSTAGE

SEX, DRUGS, AND DISTRACTION is in the middle of his performance, scanning the audience, and mentally Rolodexing the women unaccompanied by men. Once they are identified, he'll make some eye contact, enough to flirt quickly, in an attempt to assess the likelihood that one of them will accompany him back to his room. CONSCIOUSNESS feels the heat generated by SEX, DRUGS, AND DISTRACTION as the promiscuous number-crunching increases the likelihood of a very late night.

CONSCIOUSNESS: Oh, relax, would you? Let's get some sleep for a change.

SEX, DRUGS, AND DISTRACTION: I simply cannot be alone with you. You know that.

CONSCIOUSNESS: This behavior is counterproductive, useless.

SEX, DRUGS, AND DISTRACTION: Shut up, you cardigan-wearing bitch.

CONSCIOUSNESS: Cardigans are perfectly reasonable adult attire that communicate maturity and help differentiate—

SEX, DRUGS, AND DISTRACTION: Shut up. I'm busy.

SEX, DRUGS, AND DISTRACTION spots a girl with a little teardrop tattooed under one eye. She wears a minuscule amount of clothing, and she's drinking as if her glass has no bottom, as is often the wont in Vegas. This is a pretty good indicator that she is running from, and therefore toward, the same thing that he is. He meets her gaze with his own, like metal filings of opposite polarity drawn to one another through the atmosphere.

CONSCIOUSNESS (*slow and calm like a hostage negotiator*): I see what you're up to. What do you say we take a deep breath, think it through; then after the show, you and me head back to the room and get involved with that Jonathan Franzen novel you've been looking forward to. To "chase tail," as you call it, night after night is an exercise in futility.

SEX, DRUGS, AND DISTRACTION: How will I ever be involved in a real relationship if I don't try?

CONSCIOUSNESS: Surely you jest. Relationship? Really? With the face-tattooed, daddy-issue alcoholic in row eight?

SEX, DRUGS, AND DISTRACTION: I'm in the middle of a show here. And you're the one looking forward to the Franzen novel, not me. It's New Year's Eve. I'm not racing right back to the room on New Year's Eve to read *The Corrections*.

CONSCIOUSNESS: *The Corrections* is a wonderful book—

SEX, DRUGS, AND DISTRACTION: Leave me be.

CONSCIOUSNESS: Well, if I thought we could engage in a moderate amount of revelry, without you going all Keith Richards on us, I wouldn't necessarily object—

SEX, DRUGS, AND DISTRACTION: Shut up already. Does it ever end with you? I'm staying right here in the hotel. My room is eighty feet from here. To not at least try to make something happen with this girl means I have no choice but to go back to that biblically lonely room with you. I live on the road. I'm alone all day. My peak energy levels are at midnight, and yes, I like to have sex with different women. It helps me feel less detached and lonesome. It's potentially fun—though not always in practice, I admit. Best of all, it stops me from having to listen to you telling me I need to "get in touch with the real reason I'm behaving this way in the first place."

CONSCIOUSNESS: (*Laughs.*) Less "detached and lonesome"? (*Still laughing.*) Even you can't buy that! (*Gathering himself.*) I would argue that behaving that way does little *but* fuel the fire of detachment and loneliness. And as far as "getting in touch with—"

SEX, DRUGS, AND DISTRACTION: I know! I know! I'm sure it's the result of some horrible psychological void. Stand-up is generally the manifestation of dysfunction. Why else would someone feel the need to hop about in an attempt to please a roomful of strangers like some vaudevillian circus seal? I know. I get it. You're right! And you know what else? I'm going to do it any-fuckin'-way. Because the one thing you can bet your Brooks Brothers wardrobe on is that there ain't no fuckin' way I'm headed back to the room tonight to stare at the fuckin' walls with you, chewing my fuckin' ears off about the benefits of herbal tea, therapy, and Jonathan Franzen!

SEX, DRUGS, AND DISTRACTION puts an exclamation point on his mini-monologue with a sip of his double Stoli on the rocks. The audience, blissfully ignorant of this conversation, is enjoying the show.

CONSCIOUSNESS: Okay, big shot, but you know how you'll feel in the morning.

SEX, DRUGS, AND DISTRACTION: Either way, I'll be lying next to you when the sun comes up. I may as well take advantage of the fruits of my promiscuous labor, bitter as they may be.

CONSCIOUSNESS: This is not real fruit. This fruit will never make you happy—

SEX, DRUGS, AND DISTRACTION: It sure tastes like fruit!

CONSCIOUSNESS: Of course it does. Looks like it too . . . but it's not, and you know it's not. You've eaten far more than your fair share of fruit, and you're still not happy.

SEX, DRUGS, AND DISTRACTION: Maybe fruit is my thing! Isn't it possible that I just enjoy fruit?

CONSCIOUSNESS: Not to this degree, no.

Sometimes life on the road feels like the opposite of those Freddy Krueger movies. In *Nightmare on Elm Street*, Freddy comes for you when you're sleeping. On the road, he stalks you when you're awake.

3

LAS VEGAS
RIGHT AFTER THE SHOW
LAST NIGHT

Today started out typically enough—a couple of radio interviews and a spot on the local news. Press is generally annoying, but it's part of the job. In a competitive marketplace, you have to get the word out any way you can. I got the word out, and the show sold out. The people were entertained. Some of the people were really entertained, so much so that they thanked me with a couple of tabs of ecstasy and a little bag of coke. This isn't as uncommon as you might think. A fan or an appreciative audience member will walk over and leave you a little something along with a handshake. I generally turn it down—"Oh, thanks, but no thanks." Last night was not one of those times. Drugs and alcohol are not normally a big part of my life, but they were last night.

In this case, my real night begins after the show,

just before midnight. Jennifer, the female comedian I'm working with, is flirting with me, and I'm flirting back. She's sexy. *Sexy* is a word I rarely find occasion to use in conjunction with *female* and *comedian*, but tonight is an exception. It's not that attractive women aren't funny; it's just that most women who feel attractive don't end up with the personality drawbacks and lack of social options that lead to the decision to pursue comedy. I know some very funny women. Not one of them felt attractive, sexy, and/or popular as a young person. Men are not rewarded for, or penalized for, many of the things that women are. For example, the way men look matters less, creating a different social experience with different outcomes, both internally and externally. This seems to be a hot topic among white people in coffee shops and teahouses around this country, so let's put it to bed once and for all. The hot girl from high school rarely ends up in comedy for the same reason rich kids don't become professional fighters: they don't have to. Like any rule, there are exceptions, but on average, this is the way it works.

I asked Jennifer if she'd be so kind as to accompany me to the nightclub on the roof of the hotel casino. I didn't mention the name of the club, because, like the hotels that house them, they're all extensions of one another. A centipede of great views, music, men in well-tailored but tasteless button-down shirts with loud, flashy, indecipherable embroidery on the back like Rorschach tests in Braille. Women wear as little as possible. Titties everywhere, like individual entities, often inversely proportioned to the self-esteem levels of the person who bought them. Many of these people live in or near the Sun Belt but still own memberships to tanning salons. It's a snapshot of the decline of Western civilization. If you don't believe me, just ask that guy from *Jersey Shore*. He was deejaying that night. I'm not kidding.

This place is horrendous and fun. I drop one of the pink ecstasy tablets thrust upon me by that generous group of fans after the show, and Jennifer does the same. It's been a year to date since I dropped X with a girl at a nightclub. Actually, it was here at this very nightclub, with someone I liked, but she didn't like me very much. She let me fuck her anyway, a gracious gesture that was not lost on me.

Anyway, tonight I'm here with Jennifer. This is new, and somewhat intriguing, if only because it's an area where the rules are clear: NO SEX WITH FEMALE COMEDIANS. I've broken this rule a couple of times, but under very different circumstances and many years ago, when the stakes were different, and I wasn't being paid, and no one expected me to be a professional because I wasn't. The problem with rules and me is that I have a problem with rules.

"I shouldn't be doing this. I shouldn't be hitting on her. I shouldn't be attempting this, for the same reason that an office romance is taboo: it's bad business," I say to myself. "Stand-up comedy occupies a small world.

You can't help but run into one another." I continue to build my case to myself. "People talk, feelings get hurt . . . all this potential drama is never worth it when the sun comes up," I say. Ah, the hell with the sun.

A SIDE NOTE ON THE SUN

I've always resented it when television weatherpeople are disappointed in a day without sun, their permanent smiles evaporating in anticipation of the way other people will feel, as though other people feel the same things all at once. As if other people are some great monolithic weather vane. "It's going to be a wet one out there today, folks," the weatherman says with a frown, as if misery is a universally agreed-upon response to rain. I love the rain. I've got no real beef with weatherpeople, though; for what it's worth, weatherwomen have always struck me as one abusive parent away from prostitution.

UP IN THE CLUB; THE ECSTASY KICKS IN

It's New Year's Eve! I hear, "Three! . . . Two!" as the DJ counts us down. Then: "One!" Noisemakers, horns, and the people clapping all snap, crackle, and pop like a big X-rated box of Rice Krispies. Beyond the glass, fireworks illuminate the night.

It's New Year's Eve, and right now the sky looks like it's raining fire through plate glass windows as tall as dinosaurs. Absurdly vivid explosions of color rupture dry desert air. I can feel the color. I can feel it, like seeing Van Gogh's *Starry Night* for the first time in Amsterdam while tripping on mushrooms. I felt it then, like I feel it now . . . a psilocybin flashback.

Earlier in the week, I'd finished reading *The Letters of Vincent van Gogh*, a book about Vincent van Gogh's impoverished life, seen through the correspondence between him and his brother. I understood it then, but I feel it now. I can feel the epic artist crying out at the world. I can feel his pain and his sublime happiness. I felt what he was trying to say, crying out using broad brushstrokes in a language no one spoke yet. I felt him unsuccessfully attempting to communicate his experience of the universe, over and over. I heard him crying out. Crying out through the blinding, transcendent light with which he felt and saw and painted. Crying out through the language of color, and the movement of golden sunflowers in a wheat field, and spiraling green cypress and olive trees set against a swirling blue sky, and a yolk-yellow crescent moon. He cried out! Like so many artists, and housewives, and truck drivers, and electricians, and doctors, and lawyers, and unemployed single fathers, and brothers, and mothers, he cried out!

Fifty stories up, separated from the atmosphere by windows tinted with cappuccino-colored dust, the fading glow of the fireworks indicate that New Year's

Eve is now behind us. But in this moment, right now, in this second, in this millisecond, it will never end. I'm stardust, just like the building I'm in. Stardust, like the walls and the carpets, the crystal and the mirrors, the chrome and the leather, and the bad clothing— stardust. We're all stardust, nothing and everything all at the same time. Eternal life meets already dead, meets never was, meets never will be, and I couldn't be happier.

My eyes have fused with the walls of glass, like big cartoon contact lenses. I'm no longer separated from the atmosphere. I'm glued to it, and through it. Finally, I see it for what it is: an azure god, an empyrean, impressionistic masterpiece, framed by distant planets and mysteries unknown. High, high above the bereft shimmer of the skyline, I fly on painted rockets filled with gunpowder and kisses, and tears and missed birthdays, and things we wanted to say to people we loved and never did. We are one—eternal life, soundtracked by electronica and funk, techno and trance, reggae, soul, rhythm and bass.

Serotonin, dopamine, and norepinephrine high-five the pleasure receptors in my brain. My consciousness resists the oncoming traffic of euphoria, but who among us could resist the allure of the illusion, of eternal happiness? None but those of us who are already dead could possibly help themselves.

Tonight we are all stardust, turning into peacocks, riding silver surfboards over the moon, as the loneliness melts into calm pools of honey, allowing us to feel warm and a little sticky, and stuck together, and in this together, if only for a second, if only for a millisecond, if only for tonight. In the end, all we have are moments, right?

My hands, like homing pigeons, find Jennifer's hips as the bass kicks back in. White people have a special affinity for drugs in nightclubs because it makes them feel more Puerto Rican while dancing. Beats bang through six-foot-wide JBL speakers like thunderclouds hung by chains from the ceiling, and our bodies become one.

Peripherally, I spot Patricia, the Playboy Bunny who introduced me earlier. She's in civilian clothes that would make her previous outfit blush. Earlier, dressed as a bunny, she wore tights and a corset. Now she's wearing a . . . I'm not sure what it is, but if skirts were people, hers would be a dwarf. Not an average dwarf, but the kind of dwarf other dwarfs make fun of for being short. I wave to her with completely uncalled-for enthusiasm, gesturing as if I'd fallen off some ship and she were a life raft. She returns my erratic energy, teetering in our direction on candy-red five-inch pumps.

I'm not quite sure whether she's making her way toward us or away from something else. Then, like Moses through the sea, she emerges from the floor filled with writhing bodies, wrapping her arms around Jennifer and me with the misplaced vigor and enthusiasm of the intoxicated. The three of us bounce up against one another. Video images of the threesome I'm about to have whip through my mind like electromagnetic shock waves.

Fuck. A large male hand, attached to a shirt littered with skulls and bearing the label AFFLICTION, makes its way into my delicate threesome. "Yo, Trish!" he says to the bunny with the big eyes, placing an apple martini in her hand. "Fuck you been?!"

I don't like the cut of his jib, but he's been teetering his way through a crowded nightclub with a full martini like a dancing bear in a Russian circus, so I have to admire his determination. My inner stylist is appalled by his shirt, like I'm a fashion editor surveying the clothing choices of the crowd at a triple-A ball game. I can't help but wonder what drove him to make the choice to exchange valuable currency for this sartorial blunder. Ironically, the manufacturer of this shirt agrees with me. It's made by Affliction.

affliction |əˈflikshən|
noun
• something that causes pain or suffering: a crippling affliction of the nervous system.
• pain or suffering: poor people in great affliction.

It really is the perfect name for a piece of clothing no one should wear unless it was thrust upon them by conditions beyond their control. Jesus was "afflicted" by the sins of mankind. Lucky for this guy, his cross to bear consists only of cuff links and a cotton/poly blend.

The guy turns to me, introducing himself.

"Brett!" he shouts through the music.

"Dov! Like the bird, but with no *E*!" I say, pointing to myself. Saying my name this way usually prevents me from having to endure dull conversations about pronunciation.

"*What?*" he says.

"Dov, like the bird, but with no *E*!"

"*What?*"

"D-o-v!"

"*Doug?*"

"*Dov!*"

"*Doug?*"

"*Yeah, Doug!*" I say, wanting the pain to end.

SIDE NOTE ON MY NAME: I would change it if I could, but it's too late. I get so sick of the explanations of pronunciation and origin. It's an Israeli name, but I'm not Israeli. I was named after a character in the novel *Exodus*. My mother is of white Anglo-Saxon Protestant extraction. She's from California. My father is a Jew from the Bronx.

"Great show, Doug!" he says to me, extending his fist, indicating that I should do the same. It's an alternative to a handshake referred to as a *pound*.

"Thanks, man. Appreciated." I'm so happy I don't

have to fight this guy that I actually hear myself say, "Nice shirt!"

I don't know if it's where or how I grew up—probably both, combined with instinctual self-preservation data coded in through a billion years of genetic evolution—but every time a guy bigger and tougher-looking than I am says, "Good show," I think, *Great! I won't have to fight this guy.* The truth is, I already kind of like Brett. We could never be actual friends (based on his shirt, I assume that our worldviews are just too dissimilar); but that doesn't mean we can't be for an hour or so. I relate to tough guys, and even guys who just want to appear tough because they haven't thought it through.

"Yo, come sid-oun, I got bottle service ova here. Gotta bottle a Goose!" Brett shouts at me, pointing in the direction of a zebra-striped banquette studded with silver coins like rivets on an airplane that will never leave the hangar.

If you're not familiar with *bottle service*, it's when you pay seven hundred dollars—or more on New Year's Eve—for a fifty-dollar bottle of, in this case, Grey Goose, and a couple of carafes of mixers, generally orange and cranberry juices. You're then appointed a table—in reality, it's more of a coffee table—often surrounded by a couple of plushy benches, or a banquette. Congratulations, you have now become one of the honored and privileged few allowed the luxury of a small couch or banquette. This, of course, is completely ridiculous, but the club and much of pop culture, especially hip-hop, perpetuate this behavior by attaching to it cachet and social status. The sheep follow suit. Aspirational marketing at its finest.

The conversation I want to have with Brett, but won't, would go as follows:

"Hey, Brett, what did you pay for this bottle?"

"Eight hundred!" he responds proudly, making sure that I've acknowledged the status conferred by his seat, his table, and his proximity to the DJ spinning the music.

"Good deal! Let me get this straight, though. You paid twenty times what that bottle costs for the privilege of sitting down in a room with music?"

"Yup!"

"Well, if you like that deal, you're going to love this one," I say, removing a bag of Skittles from my pocket.

"What deal?" he says.

"Well, you're going to give me fifty bucks, and I'm going to allow you to chew this bag of candy while sitting in a lawn chair near the DJ booth, because that's essentially the same fuckin' deal you just made."

But Brett was nice enough to offer Jennifer and me a seat and a drink, and I'm more than happy to accept. The four of us maintain the ritual of these environs and celebrate ourselves and the evening, as though we'd received something that we deserved. We haven't, and we don't. We're lucky enough to be here at the top of this pulsating pyramid in the sky, and unlucky enough to think that this is life.

Thirty minutes later, spying the closest exit, I turn to Jennifer and raise my chin up an inch, as if to say, *Let's get the hell out of here . . . you cool with that?*

Yes, says the smirk slowly creeping across her face in anticipation of what will, inevitably, become a regret tomorrow. My warm hand, already on the upper part of her even warmer silken thigh, assumed it would be okay. I'm not the kind of guy you come with to a place like this, under circumstances like these, if you're looking for a buddy.

4

LAS VEGAS
BACK AT MY HOTEL ROOM:
HOT SCENE

We go at it. I'll spare you the details. This is my memoir, not *Penthouse Forum*, you freak. Two hours later, she passes out. She didn't do much blow, if any. I did. She's tired. I'm not. I leave the room in search of something else, anything else, anything to keep the come-down demons of solitude and self-awareness at bay. If you're at a point in your life where spending time alone feels like Chinese water torture, then Vegas is the place for you. Twenty-four hours of everything and nothing, all at the same time.

Exiting the room, I glide down the hallway and tap the Down key on the wall of the elevator bank. *Ding.* The doors open, and no sooner do I step in than I feel a pair of eyes settle upon me. "What the fuck is going on?" Slowly I turn to my left. A poster of my face, announcing my show dates and times, stares back at me.

Out loud, I hear myself say, "Shut up!" The poster hadn't said anything yet, so I think about apologizing, but don't, because I have a thing about not indulging in full-on conversations with photographs.

Strutting through the casino like a small ostrich with no feathers, I stake out a claim at the twenty-four-hour bar. The bartender approaches.

"What'll it be?" he says with a smile.

There aren't too many places in this country where you can find a smile on a bartender at three in the morning. Usually by that time, the person pushing drinks in your direction will have squandered the remainder of their joviality hours earlier. Zoning laws prevent liquor sales after 2:00 A.M. for most of America. But behind the bar at a casino in Vegas, 3:00 A.M. may as well be the middle of the day.

"Stoli on the rocks, please," I say, returning the smile and scanning the joint for anything that would talk to me—ideally, a human female. My gaze rests on a woman in her early forties, slowly sipping a mai tai. She's half-black and half-white, or some gradation thereof. I don't care. She's dressed sensibly, almost conservatively: fall colors, medium-length skirt. The exception is her heels, which are an inch higher than they should be for the dress. She's also wearing a pair of hoop earrings and puffing on a Newport. The package sends a signal: "This dress may be corporate, but I'm not."

In Vegas, hotel hookers don't dress like television hookers. Here, working girls look like real girls. It's the small things that give them away: the Newport or the hoop earrings. It's New Year's Eve at three thirty in the morning, and the woman with the Newport isn't intoxicated. She's barely sipping her drink, not drinking it. She's buying time, not partying. She invites eye contact without reservation. Even the most single-and-looking-to-mingle ladies do so with a bit of bashfulness. Also, I have a gut instinct about these things.

"How does a truffle pig know where the mushrooms are?"

"He's born with a sense of smell, that's how."

She's got miles on her face—not hard-core-drug-addict miles, just tough-life miles. I don't mind miles. And lines in faces tell stories. Like a good joke setup, I find myself wanting to stick around for the punch line. Lines increase the probability that time spent in conversation won't be a complete waste. That said, conversation is not very high on my list of needs right now.

Many guys I know wouldn't find her very attractive, but she has a nice ass. I don't see what more you need under these circumstances.

So she's not that attractive, so what? For me, a one-night stand is a one-night stand. Whether you've paid for it is immaterial. I've had sex with a number of women who, to one degree or another, make a living by way of their appearance. I've been with porn chicks, strippers, Hollywood hostesses, models, and actresses, several of whom you've seen on your television or in a film. Most of them were no more or less memorable than anyone else. Sauntering over to her stool, I think I look much cooler than I do.

"Hi. My name is Dov."

"Hi. Jazzy."

"Are you working?" I say with a look I should've been arrested for.

"Depends."

Like dogs at a park, obscenely trying to figure out whether or not they like what they smell, this goes on for a minute. She's trying to figure out if I'm a cop. I'm hoping she won't hit me up for too much, sending me back to the ATM. Then again, when you're high on coke, hundred-dollar bills feel a lot more like Monopoly money.

"How about two fifty for the hour?" I say, knowing the price would head north from there.

"Treat yo-self, don't cheat yo-self," she spits back, a rhyming utterance that has never stopped giving me at least a modicum of pleasure whenever the memory of her flawless delivery crosses my mind.

We agree on three hundred for the hour and head out across the casino floor. *Oh, fuck!* I suddenly stop, realizing that Jennifer is still sleeping in my room. Hopefully, the hotel will have a vacancy. I approach the check-in counter with the energy of a capuchin monkey on Red Bull, only to discover that they're sold out. Makes sense; after all, it's New Year's Eve.

We head in the direction of the motel across the street. NO VACANCY reads the sign. *Damn.* There are no other hotels within walking distance, at least not close enough for my lady friend in the pumps. And given the block-long line for a taxi, that's not an option either.

Here goes nothin', I think as I suggest that we head back to my room. In my brain (and some might argue, after hearing about the rest of my evening, that my brain doesn't qualify as such), I thought we could pull off the old switcheroo. That's right—the classic hooker-female-comedian-already-fast-asleep-in-your-room trade-off. I would replace a sleeping Jennifer with a wide-awake Jazzy, and no one would be the wiser.

Arriving at the door to my room, I turn to Jazzy like an attorney whispering to his client during a congressional hearing.

"Jazzy, I have to let someone out. If she sees you, pretend to be room service."

"Nigga, you crazy! I ain't pretendin' shit." Jazzy's head shot back as she sucked her teeth, chin wagging side to side, like a bobblehead doll on a bumpy road.

"Relax," I say with a manipulative smile. "Was it the room service thing? You can pretend to be the owner of the hotel, I don't care. Just don't let on that you're headed back into this room with me."

Entering the room, I find Jennifer sleeping the sleep of the not-quite-dead-but-heavily-drugged. The realization that Jennifer is not just going to hop out of bed has forced me to reconsider my original plan, so I begin to rustle about, opening and closing drawers, and doing whatever else might generate a din sufficient for waking someone well past REM. Finally, I hear, "What's going on?" I apologize for "accidentally" making too much noise. I'm not proud of what I did next. And I really mean that. It was a legitimately shameful moment. Not as shameful as what I'll do less than an hour later, but still shameful.

I ask to borrow Jennifer's room keycard, a request so absurd—given that I was already in my room—that she must have thought that she was still dreaming. She didn't even respond verbally—she just half-consciously pointed to her purse. Lucky for me, she didn't ask why, because an attempt to answer that would have sent my mind reeling, likely in the direction of a seizure.

With Jennifer's room keycard safely in hand, I head into the hallway to reconvene with Jazzy. *Now we're home-free*, I think, walking back down the hallway.

Churning through her purse as we wait for the elevator, Jazzy says, "Ah, fuck, I ran out of condoms."

Ran out? I think. Would it have killed her to find another way to say that? Even for a no-nonsense working girl, it felt a touch heavy-handed. Hurt feelings aside, I steel myself for the remainder of the mission. At this point, we're headed across the casino floor in the direction of the hotel's only twenty-four-hour store.

I push at the glass doors. They're locked. I look around for an explanation. BACK IN HALF AN HOUR says a handwritten sign, which begs the question, can a coked-out human squirrel not catch a break in this town? Jazzy shoots me a "you're on the clock" look.

In any other town, I wouldn't ask for condoms at the check-in desk, but we're in Vegas, and it's worth a shot. Jazzy follows me in the direction of a long Tuscan-marble desk. CHECK-IN, declare the big brass letters prominently hanging from the ceiling. Like any prostitute worth her salt, Jazzy doesn't approach the desk with me, but leaves a good twenty feet between us. She hangs back near a wall of Miss Piggy nickel slots—six-foot pink-and-chrome slot machines that actually oink every sixty seconds or so.

"Hello," I say to the nighttime attendant, who's dressed in a gray uniform and has an even grayer face. Her name tag reads HOPE. Ironic. She stares back at me expressionless like I haven't already said hello. She's in her late twenties, going on three hundred. She also turns out to be one of those people who makes you feel you need to apologize for asking a question. Strange, considering her very job description involves the answering of questions.

"Hi," she says, breaking the ten-second stalemate with the enthusiasm of Marie Antoinette right before the guillotine fell.

"Hi," I say for the second time. "I hope this doesn't sound strange, but I was wondering if you had . . . any . . . condoms? If you had, I mean, if you could sell me condoms?" My downcast eyes are apologizing for the awkward question.

"We don't have any condoms per se," retorted the undead.

"Per se?"

"Well, I do have an 'intimacy pack' for sale."

"What's that?"

"It's a box of condoms, but it also contains lubricant, and something else, but I'm not sure what else—"

"So you do have condoms," I say.

"I have an 'intimacy pack,'" she says, dropping a small black box on the counter like an exclamation point.

I pull some cash out of my pocket and peel off a twenty, sliding it across the marble.

"I'll take the condoms."

"You mean the 'intimacy pack'?"

"Look, Hope, right? I'm in a bit of a pinch here," I say, peering back over my shoulder to make sure Jazzy hasn't made an escape attempt.

She's there, all right, posted up against the Miss Piggy machines, tapping away at the screen of her white iPhone. *Who the hell is she texting now?* I think, but I turn back to the business at hand, meeting Ms. Macabre with renewed resolve.

"Okay, I'll just take these condoms and walk away now, but please don't ask me to use the term 'intimacy' in the context of what's about to go on."

An *oink, oink!* pierces the air, causing my eyes to land back on Jazzy for a beat, then right back to the attendant. At this point she must be wondering if my neck is just that, a neck, or a high-speed swivel, like a Humvee-mounted gun turret.

"Well, it's called—" she mumbles, about to thrust the word *intimacy* in my direction one more time.

"Well, nothing!" pops out of me. "Do you see what's waiting for me up against the pig machines?"

The first facial expression this girl has had all weekend just registered her acknowledgment of the possibility that I may not be on a honeymoon with Jazzy. The *oink, oink!* causes me to swivel my head again. Jazzy is now stretching her lower back by pulling on a slot machine handle.

"That's who I'm headed back to my room with," I say. "Clearly, we both hate ourselves. So have a little compassion, and please understand that the reason I'm refusing to use the word *intimate* is that whatever happens between me and my friend over there"—I lift my chin, gesturing in Jazzy's direction, who's released the slot handle and launched full bore into what appears to be some sort of snakelike pose—"isn't going to be intimate."

"What the hell is that?" Hope says, referring to Jazzy's unusual physicality.

"A girl can't get into a little yoga around here?" I say. "Ya know what? That's not the point—"

"What is your point?" Hope says, simultaneously amused and annoyed.

"My point is that whatever takes place between me and the snake lady over there can be described in any number of ways, with any number of words, not one of them involve using the term *intimate*. Have a great night," I say, sweeping the little black box off the counter and into my pocket with authority. Then the anger subsides—mine and hers.

Hope smiles at me. I smile back. We like each other.

I give Jazzy the "got 'em" look, and we make for the elevators.

JENNIFER'S ROOM

Finally! We're safe. We're in the room. Who knew Jennifer was so messy? I apologize to Jazzy for Jennifer's lack of tidiness.

"Sorry, I didn't realize . . . ," I say, pointing at some clothing on the floor.

Jazzy shrugs in response as if to say, *It's not even your room, and the fact that you're apologizing for this in the face of the other crimes against decency that you've committed tonight means you're an even bigger psychopath than you initially seemed.* The absurdity of this apology didn't occur to me until after I thought about how I came upon the keycard and my relationship with Jazzy in the first place. I'm standing in the hotel room of my middle act with a woman who wouldn't come near me for less than three hundred dollars, and I turn into a 1950s housewife because there are two paper cups and a pair of jeans on the floor.

Jazzy begins undressing. I take out the condoms

and suddenly realize that I never needed them in the first place because, three hours into a cocaine high, I've probably got a better shot at becoming an African dictator than achieving an erection. We get naked anyway, but because I'm ashamed to be seen in the state I'm in, I politely ask Jazzy to position herself on her knees, with her head facing the headboard, doggy-style, so that I can look at her and masturbate. Oh, I forgot to mention that I'm sitting five feet away from Jazzy in a desk chair, having aimed a floor lamp in her direction so that even if she turns around she won't be able to see me because of the spotlight shining at her. Scratching at the bottle of lube I've just removed from the intimacy pack, I peel away the plastic around the screw cap. I've been perspiring a bit, and my grip on the cap slips, causing far more lubricant to exit the bottle than was intended. Once properly lubricated, I begin twisting my flaccid piece like a lifeguard frantically performing CPR trying to bring back a drowning victim. Red-faced and a little embarrassed, still hoping for signs of life, I hear *knock! knock! knock!* "Hey, let me in!"

It's Jennifer.

Jazzy springs off the bed like Anne Frank up to the attic. Deeply involved in whatever faraway planet I'm living on at this point, I whisper at Jazzy, "Shhh . . . just wait, maybe she'll go away." *Knock! Knock! Knock! Knock! Knock!*

"I know you're in there! I can hear you! I'm calling security!" Jennifer yells through the door.

"Wait!" I screech. "I'm coming. Just a minute!"

By now, Jazzy is fully dressed. *Hookers are great under pressure*, I think, reaching for my pants.

"I'm coming!" I shout.

Within a second or two, I'm about as dressed as I can be. Flushed and breathing heavily, I fight to regain composure. At the door, Jazzy stands directly behind me. We're the world's worst SWAT team, about to breach a barrier. Jazzy gives me the "I'm ready" nod.

Bracing for what lies beyond this wooden divide, I squeeze the doorknob, and turn . . . nothing. I can't open the door. I give it another crank. Nothing. My hands are smothered in silicone-based lubricant, preventing me from executing a proper grip. Frantically, I reach for a nearby towel.

"Having some trouble with the knob!" I yell to Jennifer, desperate to buy a bit of time.

"What?" spits Jennifer, incredulous.

"The knob, it's—"

By this point, I've placed the towel between my hand and the knob, which provides me with much-needed traction. The door pops open. Jennifer's eyes are lasers. Frozen for a moment in those bewildered beams, I feel Jazzy whip by me and out the door with the alacrity of an NFL receiver headed upfield for a pass.

"What the—?" mutters Jennifer, struggling to make sense out of the sprinting hooker's silhouette.

"Sorry," I say—a life-size version of the proverbial hand in the cookie jar.

I head for the elevators, knowing that a simple "sorry" would compensate for my behavior no more than a murderer's apology leavens the spirits of the murdered. Guilt and shame, like eighty-pound sandbags, promise to make this hallway a lot longer than it actually is.

Once I've lurched my way back to the elevator, I find myself waiting for it for what seems like the tenth time tonight. After it arrives and I get in, I think about Jazzy and how if I were her, I'd be long gone right now. I think about how awful Jennifer must be feeling. By the time the elevator floor display reads LOBBY, I've put the whole incident behind me, at least until tomorrow. Cocaine, ecstasy, and alcohol don't mingle with regret.

Back at the lobby bar, wiping lubricant off my hands with a cocktail napkin, I lock eyes with a young lady seated in the very same spot occupied by Jazzy when I first encountered her. Large angel-wing tattoos adorn her naked back.

"You working?" I ask.

"That all depends," she says.

The condoms that I won't be able to use make their presence felt like lead weights in my pocket as Jazzy's replacement trails me through the casino on the way to the elevators.

"So ya make any resolutions this year?" she asks.

"Nah," I tell her.

"I did," she says. "I'm gonna cut down on sugar."

5

JERSEY
PAST AND PRESENT

At 6:00 A.M., through driving rain, I spot a black sedan sitting in front of my hotel. He's driving me to plug this weekend's gig, attempting to sell tickets via the local news program's morning show (some FOX affiliate, I think—doesn't matter which). We're due at the studio by seven, where I'm scheduled to be interviewed for a three-minute segment.

Arriving at the studio, I'm greeted by a frantic woman wearing a black headset, whom I assume to be the segment producer. If you didn't know better, you'd think something important was about to take place.

"Hi. Linda," she says briskly, introducing herself. "Dov, right?"

"Yeah."

"Is that what you're wearing?" she asks, thinly veiling her disappointment.

My energy and appearance could safely be described as "the opposite of the morning news." I'm wearing a black leather jacket and three hours of sleep. A lifetime of similarly late nights can be intuited from the expression that has taken up residence on my face. Linda shoves a lavalier mic under my shirt, grabs my hand, and drags me into the television studio like a delinquent adolescent being shown to the principal's office. Weaving through an obstacle course of wires, cables, lighting fixtures, and other people, she plants me on a couch, where I'm to meet the morning-show host, who is more often than not a man or woman with an enormous smile attached to a pair of legs and who's capable of suppressing any human emotion but glee.

The studio consists of three different sets: the news desk, the weather station positioned opposite a green screen, and the human interest / entertainment area. *Human interest* is an ironic name for the set I'm on, because it's hard to imagine an actual human finding most of this interesting. However, I'm here to plug my show and to make a living, so I swallow my pride and mind my business. The set consists of the couch I'm seated on, plastic flowers, a faux wooden coffee table, a child's finger painting, and a large papier-mâché rooster. Somebody in upper management must have suggested a country kitchen motif to their set designer, then handed him a jug of moonshine, a twenty-dollar bill, and said, "Sky's the limit!"

The host, a human light bulb in his early fifties,

pops out from behind the couch and reaches for my hand.

"Hey, Dov! I'm Cliff." He clasps my hand with the vigor of a man who orders only Ventis.

"Nice to be here."

"Gonna have a great time! Just be yourself!" he says without eye contact, while adjusting his toupee in the mirror.

"Thank you," I say, reflecting on the cataclysmic irony of the phrase *just be yourself* coming from a guy like Cliff in a place like this.

"Whoa! Missed a spot!" Cliff yelps, taking issue with his reflection. "Sally!" He careens off in the direction of the woman charged with applying his foundation. What spot could have been missed is a conundrum for better minds than mine, as Cliff's head is pancaked with more makeup than the Mexican hooker who popped my cherry.

Waiting on Cliff's reappearance, I notice the weather lady initiating her broadcast. I'm a bit dyslexic, and the smoothness with which she's able to communicate with the viewer while coordinating between the teleprompter and the green screen behind her impresses me.

Through the entrance to the studio, and much to my consternation, ten to fifteen children (not a single one of them over the age of nine), many of whom are clutching green stuffed animals, make their way into the studio and onto the bleachers opposite my couch. Linda, the harried producer, swings by with an explanation.

"Forgot to mention that the local elementary school class will be acting as our in-studio audience today," she says with a smile.

"Flying in!" cries a voice from behind the cameras. It's Cliff, bounding back into the room like a kangaroo with a pouch full of Prozac. He turns his hands into guns, blasting away at the kids. The children smile. He's already won them over. Pivoting on one heel, Cliff turns his guns on me, sending a few rounds in my direction before stealing the seat next to me.

I feel a heightened sense of existential angst. *Is this really my life?*

Once settled, he shoots a thumbs-up at the producer, who cues the camera guys. "Three, two, one . . . ," calls Linda as the light on camera four turns green. Impossibly, Cliff's smile has become even more brilliant.

"Hey, everybody, we're back . . . and joining us today, comedian Dov Davidoff!" Cliff waits for applause from the studio audience that never comes.

I can feel the children wondering what I am. I'd like to talk to the kids and involve them in a way that would allow us to learn more about one another, but I have only three minutes to do a couple of jokes and plug my gig.

"So what's happening in your life, Dov?" Cliff asks at a volume that feels more accusatory than inquisitive.

At this point, I have to steer things in the direction of my material; I don't see anything organically funny happening between Cliff and me.

"Well, I'm having relationship issues," I say, setting up a joke. I know it's not going to be kid-friendly, but my job is to sell a few tickets to the adult viewers, not to appeal to the comedic palate of a fifth grader.

"You ever love somebody, but you don't like 'em?" I say to the camera, which is now situated between me and the kids, leaving the children with the impression that I'm speaking directly to them. "You know, like, 'I love you, but I don't like the way I feel when you're in the room' . . . 'I love you, but if I were this much more healthy'"—I hold my fingers a paper's thickness apart—"'I would get the hell out of this relationship yesterday.' Love is like a drug, the highs are high, the lows are low. If love were a drug, people would be, like, 'Stay away from that stuff . . . you can lose your house!'"

You can hear a pin dropping on wet cotton. Even Cliff's irrepressible smile has lost a few watts. The children are visibly uncomfortable or at least confused. So am I. I shouldn't be here, or they shouldn't be here. Somebody shouldn't be here.

"O-kay," says Cliff, doing his best to send us to commercial without communicating the lead balloon of awkwardness to the viewers at home. "Back atcha inna couple of minutes," he says, waving at the camera with a wink, or a twitch—who can tell with eyelashes that active?

The producer approaches me and asks that I follow her over to a carpeted area in front of a lime-colored wall. Simultaneously, she waves eight or nine children over from the bleachers and informs us that we're all going to be dancing our way back from commercial, as a "bumper" into the next segment (the same way *The Today Show* will use shots of their outdoor crowd holding handwritten signs before and after a commercial break). I think she's kidding. She's not. This strikes fear into my heart for two reasons: One, the last thing in the world I want to do, under the glare of floodlights, in a newsroom, at seven in the morning, on three hours of sleep, is dance. Two, the last thing in the world these children want to do, under the glare of floodlights, in a newsroom, at seven in the morning, is dance with me.

"Three, two, one . . . we're back!" announces the producer as some rhythmless musical version of maple syrup pours through the speakers. The children, like dancing particles in a centrifuge, drift toward the perimeter, leaving a conspicuous gap in the center that's filled by me, alone. Like Jesus on the cross, I want to yell out, "God, God, why have you forsaken me?" Instead, I raise my arms in the air and gyrate my hips a bit, biting down, with increasing discomfort, on the bitter herb of commerce, compromise, and responsibility.

6

JERSEY
THE BEGINNING
OF IT ALL

On the ride back to the hotel, I stare at the brake lights of the car in front of us. They're beautifully obscured by mist created by wheels on wet pavement at sixty-five miles an hour. I'm transported back to the place I so desperately longed to leave: my own childhood. My earliest memories aren't really memories at all, but vague feelings—of shame, confusion, sadness, joy, hatred, love, and some fun as well.

I grew up in an old farmhouse with a dirt driveway in Englishtown, New Jersey, not too long a drive from where we were taping. Not too far from where Bruce Springsteen grew up. Do away with any images of a picket fence and rolling hills dotted with apple trees. My mother did have something of a green thumb, but our main crop was dysfunction, and periodically, marijuana.

Located directly across the street was the sordid touchstone of my existence, my father's family business. Jack's Auto Wreckers was a junkyard named after my grandfather, consisting of acres of twisted metal and old cars, many of them stacked one on top of the other. On one side of my house was a long, narrow building in various stages of disrepair, which my father "rehabbed," converting it into a retail storefront. Given the demographic in the area and the overall desirability of the space, it was leased to a guy who sold discount tools and VHS porn. On the other side of the street were houses filled with working-class people. People without educations who lived check to check—the kinds of people who inhabit early Bruce Springsteen lyrics. My house was burglarized two or three times, and my bicycle was stolen more than that. I was the last of my family to live there. At the age of seventeen, I moved out, at which time my father leased my boyhood home to an unlicensed electrician named Phil, who had a long ponytail and a penchant for Taco Bell. There were little plastic hot-sauce packets everywhere, except, of course, on the kitchen counter, upon which sat a motorcycle engine Phil was forever tinkering with. The house has since been demolished, and the land on which it sat has been turned into a parking lot.

Located in the junkyard, a couple of hundred feet from where I lived, was the house where my grandparents lived for many years until a couple of guys decided to rob the place. The burglars were former employees of my grandfather's who worked at the junkyard. In the dead of night, they entered through a window and attacked my grandparents with hammers while they slept. The amount of blood that covered the walls of their bedroom was more suggestive of ritual murder than burglary. My grandparents had to have metal plates inserted into their heads. They lived but were never the same.

The area, about an hour south of New York City, was relatively rural but loud and busy during the day; tow trucks, flatbeds, and forklifts would flow in and out of the junkyard. The whine of the crushers, reducing cars to the height of a footstool, could be heard all day long. Less than a mile away was a drag-racing strip. Three-hundred-mile-an-hour top-fuel funny cars producing seven thousand horsepower would create artificial thunder on weekend nights.

Below our house was a basement apartment. Gordon lived there. For the better part of a decade, I thought the guy was terribly nervous, not realizing that his shaky hands were the result of alcoholism. He worked nights at a local factory, and I don't remember him having ever received a single visitor during the day. In hindsight, I wish I'd tried to talk to him more, reducing, if only fractionally, what must have been a profound loneliness. But I was too young to understand. He never bothered me, and I returned the favor.

Gordon wasn't our only basement resident. There

was Walter, a diminutive birdlike man who had run afoul of the law. I never asked him what happened, and he never brought it up. He needed a place to lie low but couldn't afford rent. He refused to provide a social security number and was fearful and mistrusting. Smelling an opportunity, my father immediately poured a concrete floor next to the washer and dryer in the basement and welcomed Walter into our home with open arms, contingent upon his working under the table at a laughably low wage. Inexpensive labor and the avoidance of employer-funded payroll taxes were much more likely to put a smile on my father's face than any holiday. That said, my father did more for Walter than most people would have, putting himself at risk by hiring him in the first place. Walter didn't seem unhappy, given the circumstances, avoidance of incarceration, and a roof. He was a peaceful soul who spent what little time he had, when he wasn't slaving away in the junkyard, listening to jazz on a small transistor radio he'd taken from the trunk of an abandoned car. On weekends, he'd take the bus to a local theater, buy a single ticket, and go movie-hopping. He would talk to me about the films he saw—what he liked and didn't like about them. Sometimes he would share stories with me about the junkyard and the men he worked with, and how they could be a bit brutish for his taste. My feelings for him are as warm as those I have for anyone from that period of my life.

Behind our house was a one-bedroom shack that

my father rented out to a couple of hippies. As you may have gathered, my father was something of a hustler; he'd sublet an empty coffee cup if he could find a tenant. I don't remember much about the hippies, other than they had a daughter, walked around naked from time to time, and smoked a lot of pot.

7

JERSEY
MY MOTHER

After a period of consideration that could only be described as brief, my mother began growing marijuana in the front yard, even though she didn't smoke it. Her crop flourished. Tall, fuzzy, emerald spires peeked over the front fence, announcing their presence to passersby. Trash bags full of the stuff were kept on the porch. My mother wasn't concerned about laws, though she was about rules. Rules were created for people, by people; laws were bureaucratic.

"I grew it for my friends. None of this is meant to be sold!" my mother explained to the authorities after her arrest. The lawmen wore looks of skepticism. On some level, my mother must have assumed that the lead investigator would come to his senses and angrily admonish his inferiors. Like, "Hey, idiots, put down the cuffs and the fifty-pound bags of herb. This is *gift* weed!"

My parents were divorced after two years of marriage. I don't know how long it takes to finalize a divorce, but if there had been any logic in the universe, initial proceedings would have begun within an hour of "I do." The fact that they decided to remain living together in that same house for the following ten years still confounds me. My mother lived upstairs, my father down. To describe the atmosphere as acrimonious does the word *acrimony* a great disservice. It was a mini–Middle East, without all the levelheaded thinking. From my earliest memories, my father hated my mother.

You're probably asking yourself how my parents' fairy-tale romance began. Here's how: my father was an uneducated Jewish guy, originally from the Bronx, who met my mother, an intellectual, hippie WASP from California, when she was on her way to teach piano in India and stopped off to visit a close friend of hers, who at the time was living in New Jersey. My mother's friend was a lesbian and the proud owner of a monkey. Back then, society's silent contract with gay primate owners often required that they take up residence in places one tends to describe as "off the beaten path." My father happened to be the owner of a rustic rental property on such a path. It would eventually become the house that I was born and raised in.

I don't know why they married. They fell in love, I

guess. On the surface, it seems as though they should never have found themselves in the same place at the same time, let alone married to each other, but as I've gotten older and made my own mistakes, I feel like I understand more. I know what it's like to fall in love with what you want, without really knowing what you need, or maybe it is what we needed at the time. Maybe that's what they call growing up.

If my mother were to write a memoir, it could be entitled *Right War, Wrong Battle*. Being near her often provides me with the opportunity to feel reverence and frustration simultaneously. I'll give you an example. A year ago, she invited some friends of hers to dinner at a swanky Midtown Manhattan hotel I was staying at. After sniffing around the hotel, she realized that there was a picnic-type area with outdoor tables, so she decided to scrap dinner plans and just pick up some crackers, hummus, and a pint of lentils. She didn't bring a fork or a knife or napkins. She didn't let anyone know that they'd be eating hummus and lentils and little else. Her friends arrived, along with a couple of mine. It was Saturday night, and we were all dressed for dinner and a night on the town. I could see the creeping disappointment on everyone's faces as it slowly dawned on them that not only would they be eating nothing but hummus and lentils for dinner but they'd be doing so with their hands. I shot my mother a look like, "*No forks?*" She responded with something along the lines of "There's too much waste in this country. In India, everyone eats with their hands." *Right War*: she's right—there is far too much thoughtless waste in Western culture in general and America specifically. *Wrong Battle*: it's Saturday night. Forcing a tableful of unsuspecting friends to dig hummus out of a container like bears sifting through garbage may not be the clearest path to a greener planet.

8

JERSEY
THE LAND

My mother was immersed in a cult called "the Land" for much of my childhood. As far as I can tell, they were engaged in a search for meaning, principally through Eastern religious philosophy and communal living. I've got no beef with the pursuit of spirituality—we can all benefit from a journey inward—but I've never understood why the path to enlightenment is jammed with people wearing sandals and clothing made from hemp. Is finding God more difficult with a closed-toed shoe or a shirt that doesn't look like it was cut from a potato sack? Is there something in the ancient texts about morality's dress code? "All ye righteous must appear vaguely homeless and carry a hacky sack." Is God waiting at the gates, like, "What are you wearing?"

"Adidas."

"Not in my house." Thunderclap. "Off to hell, where everyone lives in pain and stylish leather."

For my mother and her cult, Hilda was the focus of their admiration. I was told that "Hilda was never born, and Hilda will never die." Hilda is dead now, but that's not the point. She was of half-Indian extraction and wore a blue robe of sorts. There was an "otherness" about this woman, an ethereal quality often associated with charisma. I don't remember the first time I saw her, but I do remember feeling the energy in the room change when she entered it. People continued about their business, but in a more muted, deliberate way. As is true of seeing a police car in your rearview mirror, her presence heightened everyone's awareness of themselves.

Hilda was special, and I can see why people followed her. She was a leader. We all need leaders, but those leaders need to be reminded that they are in fact people. Otherwise, hearing of voices and shirts with higher-than-usual collars will likely follow.

Hilda would lecture near St. Patrick's Cathedral in Manhattan, where most of her followers lived. Under Hilda's directives, the Land was created. The Land was just that—a hundred or so acres of land located about four hours north of New York City, where all the members would pool their resources and grow their own food—vegetarians only, please. In addition to the preparation of an enlightened menu, meditation and the construction of earth-integrated housing would occupy most of their waking hours. Also, I remember some hot-coal walking, telekinetic spoon-bending, and some discussion about whose "third eye" was really open. Also, freeze-dried food would be purchased and stored. Out-of-wedlock sex between members was taboo. I thought this was odd, as I've always considered informal sleeping arrangements to be among the only definitive upsides of cult life.

I interacted with these people enough to know that they were well-meaning, industrious, and thoughtful. They worked to cultivate their corner of the world into a place that made sense to them. As I said, I harbored no ill will toward them. On the contrary, I found the level of conviction necessary to create and sustain the Land courageous, unique, and even beautiful. My issue with their arrangement was not that its goal was to create an alternative to godlessness or to spurn a shallow, materialistic culture. My objection had more to do with what they claimed to be saving their members from: nuclear Armageddon.

There's nothing crazy about mistrusting governments, with the horrific End-of-Days nuclear potential they possess. This was especially true during the Cold War of my childhood. But there *is* something crazy about thinking that, come crunch time, you'll be protected by a "spiritual force field" enveloping "the Land" in a protective coating of "rainbow." Crazier than that by half was the notion that they'd be able to make it out of New York City as the bombs plunged from the sky. The Land was located four hours away. I don't know if you've ever tried leaving Midtown Manhattan after a Knicks game, but I'm thinking that thermonuclear warheads colliding with skyscrapers have the potential to create some backup in and around the bridges and tunnels. Again, my beef was not philosophical but logistical. One: you're not going to make it to the Land; two: if you do, your predilection for open-toed footwear probably won't protect you from the effects of nuclear fallout.

9

JERSEY SAI BABA

When I was eleven, my mother brought my brother, Orion, and me with her to India. For her, this was a pilgrimage, not a vacation. I hated my life. My hair was cut in such a way that several Indian street vendors and a bus driver were convinced that I was a girl. "Come into my store, and bring your daughter," said one of the shopkeepers. It was a decade before I could laugh about that.

We set out for the village of a famous Indian holy man known as Sai Baba. We piled onto a bus so crowded, it felt like the only separation between its occupants was mental. This was the eighties, and travel by bus in India was second in discomfort only to outdoor surgery during the Civil War. I'm reminded of something I read in a book, set in Bombay, in which the author observed that private physical space was a luxury that many of the world's poor could not afford. I can't speak Hindi, but I'm pretty sure several Indians kept repeating the phrase *Can you believe this shit?*

Finally we were there, Sai Baba's village. Sai Baba wore a large afro and had a penchant for dark sunglasses and the color orange—or, as holy men like to call it, "saffron." I'm convinced that many of this man's perceived spiritual powers were derived from the delirious and despairing state in which his followers arrived upon exiting the bus. Who wouldn't be a bit more prone to belief in that state? Many religious visions have been seen and voices heard in the context of deprivation. A lack of food and water, combined with physical exertion and limited sleep, tends to manifest in strange ways. From Jesus to Muhammad and nearly everyone in between, deprivation may have contributed to visions and delusional perceptions. Point being, if there had been a Burger King in the desert two thousand years ago, Muslims, Jews, and Christians might have less to argue about.

Our accommodations were rudimentary. We slept on the floor. It was kind of like a four-floor hotel without walls or rooms. One concrete slab suspended above another. But it was warm, and we didn't care—that is, until my brother fell asleep. I'm not sure which one of us awoke first, but Orion's head had become a thriving ant colony. Apparently, he had munched himself to sleep with a chocolate bar. Orion, like many ten-year-olds, didn't realize that falling asleep with your lips coated in a blanket-thick layer of Three Musketeers was something of a no-no in these parts.

I never got to see Sai Baba up close, but my mother did. She regaled us with an account of how Sai Baba could cause *vibhuti* (holy ash) to materialize in his hands out of thin air. He could also conjure small pieces of jewelry, I was told. Given the abject poverty surrounding us, you'd think he would've conjured up something valuable, but apparently God had limited him to the non-precious metals.

Sai Baba had no direct association with Hilda or the Land, but he had many thousands of devotees who believed deeply in his abilities and guidance as a "holy man." They believed he'd been ordained by something greater than ourselves, and they invested their dreams and desires, and most important, their hope, in him. They believed he was a conduit through which God could, and would, speak.

They were wrong—and for that I feel a deep and lasting sadness. Not just for them but for mankind. They paid the price of the desperate and the gullible. We'll give anything to believe, including our identities. We want so desperately to believe that we will ourselves into deception. Holy men, priests, and politicians, and the false promises of materialism and celebrity and anything else we can wrap our frightened hands and minds around.

My mother has been to India several times, and on one of those trips, she had a near-death experience. If you're going to consume water in India, it must first be boiled to eliminate harmful bacteria. In her case, it was boiled, but the ice cubes in the water hadn't been. She became so ill that she thought she might die. Badly dehydrated, almost delirious, she asked herself the following question: "If I were given a choice between a personal introduction to God right now or a cold glass of Tropicana orange juice, which one would I choose?" After a short period of deliberation, she went with the OJ.

After arriving home, a neighbor of mine asked me where I'd been.

"India," I said.

"Where's that, Queens?" he asked.

That was the last time I tried to talk about that experience with anyone I grew up around. There was to be no discussion of the Land or India for many years to come. I can barely find a way to communicate the isolation I sometimes feel now, as an adult, let alone the intensity of the isolation I felt as an eleven-year-old returning from Sai Baba's ashram.

10

JERSEY
MY FATHER

I returned from India to the almost equally strange environment of the junkyard. The next morning, I made my way up the junkyard's dirt driveway. I could hear my father yelling. This doesn't mean he's angry, just that he's communicating. I opened the door to the "office"—basically a cargo trailer with windows and a door, set on cinder blocks. My father was explaining to a couple of befuddled customers who'd made the mistake of offering him a cup of coffee why he was unwilling to accept.

"Do me a favor," he said, his hands becoming stop signs. "I don't need any friends. You two bring me cawffee at the beginning of the day, cawffee costs you fifty cents a cup. End a da day, you want two hundred off the price of a motor, cuz you're my buddy. Cawffee costs you fifty cents, costs me two hundred. Keep ya fuckin' cawffee. I don't need any friends!"

Though this sounds harsh, my father was able to communicate it in a way that prevented the customers from being too deeply offended. Oftentimes he did it in a way that would actually cause the customer to laugh. Like a comedian working the crowd, he needed to let people know he was in control without actually insulting or becoming overtly confrontational. It was more like he was saying, "Me and you are cool, but when it comes time to pay, I don't want any song and dance."

I learned many life lessons in this manner from my father. He'd often take me with him when negotiating the purchase of a used car. Generally, this would take place behind someone's house or in their front yard or right on the street. The same thing happened every time: the seller would greet us, sometimes with a smile, and then, after a minute or two, the seller would become withdrawn and sullen, as the grim reality of being paid a fraction of what they'd expected set in. On the ride back to the junkyard, my father would say, "Whatever they have, you don't need." What he meant was that when negotiating with anyone who wants to sell you something, your job is to convince them that you don't really want it, but for a ridiculously low price, you'd be willing to take it off their hands, seeing as you "already drove all the way the hell out there."

"If they have an automatic, you got plenty of automatics. You need a standard shift, a stick. If they have a standard shift, who da fuck wants that? We need automatics."

Another time, seated with him at a diner, I was admonished for ordering a cup of soup.

"Look again at the menu," he said.

"What?" I said.

"What's a cup a soup cost?"

"Two bucks," I said. (It was the 1980s.)

"What's a bowl cost?" he shot back.

"Two fifty."

"For another fifty cents, you get twice as much. Never order a cup; that's how they get ya."

"Okay," I said, reaching for a piece of bread.

"Lay off the bread," he'd say.

"Why?"

"That's how they get you."

"What?"

"Nothin', just save room for your food."

The bread paranoia never made much sense to me, but I still live by almost every other lesson he taught me.

My father always said, "Believe none of what you hear and only half of what you see." He'd also say, "When buying a car, you look under the hood, not at the paint job like a moron." A simple concept, but take a look around: How many people have bought into an idea, or a product, or a person, without "looking under the hood"? If everyone looked under the hood, much of what is known about contemporary business models (certainly the ones based on aspirational marketing, such as nightclub bottle service, three-hundred-dollar jeans, and Kim Kardashian) would have to be rethought.

Over and over, these lessons were spot-welded to my consciousness. Everything was a cost-benefit analysis to my father. He grew up poor, and the ability to recognize value would differentiate him from those who stayed poor. Figuring out who was "full of shit" and who wasn't was, for my father, the difference between whether or not you had heating oil in the winter.

11

JERSEY
MY GRANDFATHER

Though my father could be abrasive, he had the stolid demeanor of a diplomat compared to my grandfather, who was born and raised on the Lower East Side of Manhattan when it was still a ghetto. My grandfather was born with a cigar in his mouth and died the same way. He didn't like me, but then again, he didn't like anybody, so I didn't take it personally. He still put in a few days a week at the junkyard when I was a kid, so I saw him pretty regularly throughout my early life. He referred to me only as "Duffy." This was not a grandfatherly nickname bestowed upon me, say, as the sun set during a life-lessons-through-fly-fishing trip. He simply couldn't wrap his head around the idea that my parents named me Dov, so he called me something else. We never had an actual conversation, and I can only remember him addressing me directly on two occasions.

The first was an accusation of tool theft, a crime he regularly accused any number of people of, up to and including family members and the recently deceased. The second, and more heartfelt, was when he stood close to me, almost shoulder to shoulder, pointing in the direction of several Latino gentlemen.

"Duffy," he said, "watch the Puerto Ricans; they steal."

My grandfather was convinced that the world wanted whatever he had, and if he weren't looking, they'd put it in their pockets and walk away. Paranoia was his passion. As is true of all the ethically challenged, it was his own nature that made him so acutely aware of others' potential for larceny. Every Sunday, several twenty-dollar bills would disappear from the register, so my father hired my brother to keep an eye on our grandfather. The bills stopped disappearing.

He used to wish brain cancer on his brother. "He should drop dead of brain cancer, that son of a bitch bastard what he is, that cocksucka what he is!" All expletive-laced insults were curiously followed by the phrase *what he is*. These diatribes were not reserved for his brother alone but for anyone and everyone. Buddhist monk–like, he repeated his mantra until words blended into sounds without meaning: "Son of a bitch bastards what they are. Cocksuckas what they are."

A quarter mile up the road, my grandfather's sister (my great-aunt, though I don't remember ever having met her) was the proud owner of a hot dog business, which consisted of a truck, through the window of which she sold tubes of what could hardly be described as meat or even food. It was a moderately profitable business nonetheless. As the story goes, some guy tried to muscle in on her turf with a competing truck. She explained to the gentleman that she'd been there for years, and even though she didn't own the land on which the truck sat, he should respect her seniority. In short, "There is no room for the both of us, and I was here first." The man didn't listen. She had him killed. Apparently, he was blown up in his hot dog truck. This happened before I was born, so my account is second-hand. When I asked my father whether it was true, he paused for a moment, then said, "Who knows?" Meaning it was true enough to be a subject not fit for discussion. Again, I didn't know her, but if she was anything like my grandfather, I'm sure the explosion was loud.

12

JERSEY
BIG BILL

I felt safe in the junkyard. It was my home. I don't
know that I *belonged* there, but I'm positive I belonged
anywhere else even less. The men who worked there
knew me and were nice to me. They didn't care that my
sneakers had dirt on them, because theirs did too.
Most were functionally illiterate, some entirely so. Many
were felons. One guy did seven years in prison for
running a chop shop; another was incarcerated for a
sex crime; yet another for grand larceny. The list goes
on. I was told that one of the men who worked there
had been caught fucking a chicken. Ironically, he was
made fun of for being semi-retarded and toothless, but
I don't remember anyone bringing up the chicken
much. I can't confirm that he was ever with a chicken,
but the fact that I couldn't dismiss it speaks volumes.

The junkyard could be a pretty dangerous place,

and people got hurt from time to time. Cuts, fires, and fractures all come with the territory of petroleum, iron, and acetylene torches (6,300-degree torches that cut through quarter-inch steel like a metal blade through ripe fruit). I was with my father when he endeavored to haul a two-and-a-half-ton safe to the local scrapyard.

"Big Bill!" my father yelled. "Give me a hand, would ya?"

Big Bill, a large, muscular man in his thirties, wrapped heavy-gauge steel cable around the body of the safe. This cable was attached to a powerful winch, secured to a flatbed truck. My father pulled a lever under the bed, engaging the hydraulic pistons, allowing him to lower the long steel bed onto which the safe would be dragged upward. The next lever he pulled engaged the winch, causing the cable to tighten like a boa slowly winding around its prey. Miraculously, this five-thousand-pound block of metal lurched forward. The sounds of metal on metal ground painfully through my eardrums as the rigid, astonishingly tense cable snorted in the face of gravity. I couldn't believe this kind of weight allowed itself to be induced into movement by machines created by mere humans. Then a loud snap fractured the air, reverberating through my stomach. It was the feeling you get when faced with the wrong side of a pistol barrel.

Big Bill's legs jutted out from the ground beneath the safe, as if someone had accidentally left them behind. The first dead body I'd ever seen was attached to a pair of work boots.

13

JERSEY
A MOVEABLE FEAST

Despite the danger, the junkyard could also be a lot of fun. My brother and I would take old cars destined for the crusher and slam them into one another in a derby of destruction, and we'd erupt with laughter. We sawed off the barrel of a twelve-gauge shotgun. I fired it at the rear window of a car. The front windshield is actually two pieces of glass, between which sits a layer of adhesive, making it shatterproof, and consequently much less fun to shoot. But the rear window blast created paroxysms of glass, like exploding rain, providing me with a level of joy—bordering on exultation—that I haven't known since. I'd cradle a .22-caliber rifle in my arms, pretending to be something I wasn't, and take aim at the keyholes in car doors.

A. E. Hotchner, the author of a biography of Ernest Hemingway, remembered a conversation he once had with the great writer. Hemingway said, "If you are lucky enough to have lived in Paris as a young man, then wherever you go for the rest of your life, it stays with you, for Paris is a moveable feast." The junkyard was my Paris, and the lessons I learned there, the stories I heard, the experiences I had, and the cast of characters I would come to know—and not know— were my feast.

There was Deaf George, the tow-truck driver who, unable to hear horns or someone yelling, regularly backed up into cars, parts, people, and anything else guilty of assuming it had been heard. It always struck me as strange that everyone insisted on calling him Deaf George. He was the only George that worked there, so there was no need to differentiate him from another.

Black Lou, on the other hand, was one of two guys name Lou employed there at the time, and he was the blacker of the two. Black Lou grew up in Jersey, but his accent was so strong and he spoke with such Ebonics-laced rapidity that he may as well have been from another planet, because no one understood him. Black Lou was blessed with the patience of a twelfth-century cloistered monk. I'd never known anyone else who could tolerate my grandfather's negativity for longer than a few minutes at a time. They were an odd pair, reminding me of something I'd seen on YouTube about a friendship between an Asian elephant and a stray dog, or another about a young hippopotamus and an elderly giant tortoise. Like the dog and the elephant, Black Lou and my grandfather's relationship was not based on verbal communication or any other similarity that I could make out but something more primal: an ancient fellowship, a sort of spiritual complementing.

They only had one conversation as far as anyone could tell, and they would have it over and over again during the course of a single day, as that day turned into weeks, months, and years. Black Lou would lean up against an old car within earshot of my grandfather.

"Son of a bitch bastards what they are," my grandfather would mutter, his cigar shivering with invective.

"Sho, you right," Black Lou would respond coolly.

"Cocksuckas what they are."

At this point, Black Lou would nod *yes*, but without head movement. Using only his eyelids, which would pitch up and down, ever so slowly, like molasses covering the bottom of a clear glass, he was able to communicate agreement.

"Son of a bitch bastards what they are . . ." And so it would go as the bond between the hippo and the tortoise took root in the oil-soaked ground of our junkyard.

A guy named Gus worked in the office for a bit— that is, until he was caught stealing. Gus was in his late sixties, wore Coke-bottle glasses, and had a predilection for shorts sans underwear, no matter the weather. People made fun of him because one of his balls used to hang out whenever he sat down. Whenever this testicular oversight was brought to my father's attention, he'd sneak behind Gus and slap the dangling globe with a metal yardstick. Whether the other ball had gone missing, and how, was a subject of debate.

Gus was replaced by a cross-eyed biker with a bum leg, named Paul, who introduced my father to the wonderful world of freebasing cocaine. Paul's wife, Tanya, an unattractive woman with an intensely raspy voice, would flutter through the office from time to time. Her voice reminded me of a quiet chain saw, and one day I asked my father about it. Though he was busy answering calls, he put the phone down, looked solemnly in my direction, and said, "Swallowing too much cum," before returning to his call.

Fat Jimmy was indeed fat. He didn't work in the junkyard but was something of a fixture anyway. He wore short-sleeved button-down shirts and a gold rope chain. The Playboy dice and green-tree air freshener that hung from the rearview mirror of his 1982 Oldsmobile Cutlass Supreme let everyone know he was a ladies' man. In addition to being a Lothario, he was top dog at a local auto-body shop. But he had no compunction about spending hours traversing the rotting floorboards of the junkyard office, regaling anyone who would listen with sordid tales of late-night coitus and the odd blow job he "caught" in the back of his Cutlass. Whenever I saw those black-and-white dice bouncing their way up the junkyard's dirt driveway, I was filled with the anticipation of a boy awaiting stories, told by a man who shouldn't be telling them in the first place.

Nothing of junkyard life impressed me more than the hands of the men who worked there. Like sepia photographs hanging on the walls of my memory, their hands were those of men who truly work for a living. Not work like I work, or probably like you work. I mean work like outdoors three hundred and something days a year, no health care, half your paycheck under the table, living check to check, "how do I feed my family if I break my arm" work. Work like sunrays-multiplied-by-metal-hot-enough-to-sear-skin work. Work like winter's-frost-permeating-your-bone-marrow-more-deeply-with-each-finger-numbing-turn-of-the-wrench-as-you-struggle-to-break-free-ice-encased-chassis-bolts-in-an-attempt-to-extract-the-value-from-an-old-Chevy-on-its-way-to-the-crusher work.

14

JERSEY '70S PORN

I shared with these men the closest approximation to friendship I'd ever experienced. Befriending the children I sat next to at school was not an option for me. My classmates were mean and provincial. They looked down on me for growing up in a junkyard, having a funny name, and being a chubby kid with dirty sneakers who wore secondhand clothes. They didn't like me because I was half-Jewish, or because my mother was a hard-core hippie in an area where there were none.

Never was this more apparent than when I sat down for lunch. I was profoundly uncomfortable shoulder to shoulder with my classmates, smugly chewing their way through Wonder Bread sandwiches pulled from neat little ziplocked baggies, made for them by coupon-cutting mothers who used Pine-Sol and didn't read books. When I stared into my lunch sack, pita bread—the bane of my existence—stared back at me. However, I was famished and had little choice. Like a survivalist forced to eat his own shoe leather, I removed the terrible wheat-colored disc from my paper bag. In many cases it was stuffed with sprouts and a whole tomato. It was as though someone had turned seventies porn into a sandwich. Given my classmates' expressions, I may as well have yanked out some raw fish and a pair of chopsticks, but not before donning a kimono and some geisha whiteface. I was already the subject of derision, but the pita bread really helped take things to the next level.

I remember telling my mother, "This pita has got to come to an end."

"It's healthy," she'd say to me.

Healthy, I thought. *Is it healthy to be hated? Is that healthy?* I fantasized about shooting a few of those little motherfuckers I went to school with. The cops would ask my mother, "What happened? Why did your son open fire on a tableful of ten-year-olds?"

"I don't know," my mother would say. After a beat, she'd be forced to admit, "I guess he went crazy . . . but he had low cholesterol."

Other kids made fun of me for having full lips or a bad haircut. One pasty-faced punk accused me of "picking through the cars" with my "dirty-Jew father" after accidents, but before we towed them back to the junk-yard. This was not the case. Those were impounds and were to be sealed until the owner, or a representative from their insurance carrier, came to retrieve them.

Many vehicles that ended up in the yard had been totaled as the result of a devastating collision, often leaving the occupants seriously injured or dead. On a number of occasions, I watched my father on a humid summer night, breathing heavily, sweat glistening on his forehead in the glare of police lights. He'd be toiling in and around the steering column of a blood-soaked sedan, attempting to break free the front wheels, allowing the vehicle to be towed from the rear. Under these circumstances, removing valuables would have been beyond his comprehension. Whoever said there is no honor among thieves didn't know my father.

One time I remember the lunch bell reverberating through my fifth-grade classroom, driving me out of the room and into the busy hallway. As I was energetically shuffling across the cafeteria floor, my foot caught the edge of an uneven tile, sending me head over heels into the corner of a crowded table. A pretty, popular, flaxen-haired girl whom I had something of a crush on squealed with laughter as everyone turned to witness the commotion.

"Oh, look!" she squealed. "It's Dov! The bird that's too fat to fly."

Her timing was excellent, though I had some difficulty appreciating it at the time, as there was limited oxygen in my lungs and a stabbing pain in my chest. Crying on the inside, I left the building and ate my pita bread in the shade of a small tree, alone, like a political exile, banished from the kingdom of children.

Fret not, kind, compassionate reader, for later in life, I'd punch her bully of a boyfriend in the face, and a couple of weeks after that, I'd fuck her in the back seat of my buddy's Camaro, but we're not there yet.

I felt ugly, awkward, isolated, and deeply misunderstood. The deck had been stacked long before I'd arrived. Years later, in high school, I'd be one of the feared and socially sought-after, but again, we're not there yet.

15

JERSEY FRANKENSTEIN

I used to miss the school bus on purpose. I couldn't bear my classmates' twisted little faces as the early-morning sun poured through the greasy glass panels with their greasy little palm prints plastered all over them. I hated the uncomfortable, shit-colored, plastic bench seats. As the bus pulled away without me, I'd march up the junkyard driveway.

"Dad, missed the bus. Can you give me a lift?"

In the event that he couldn't drive me, which was often, he'd summon Toothless Frank, a man in his forties who occupied a position on my I-can't-take-it-anymore scale somewhere right below pita bread. As you may have imagined, Toothless Frank was not a big dental hygiene advocate. And yet, even though he had not a tooth in his mouth, he could tear through an apple with the best of them.

"Hop in!" he yelled, pointing in the direction of his car, a patchwork quilt on twenty-six-inch racing slicks with no muffler. It was a remarkable jerry-rigged assortment of body parts from other vehicles—the hood and the trunk from one, quarter panels from another, fenders from yet another, all colliding in a diaspora of primer gray, polka-dotted throughout with large splotches of off-white Bondo. Imagine a fucked-up old muscle car with an inoperable case of Rocky Mountain spotted fever. Like in Mary Shelley's *Frankenstein*, this monster was the result of an unorthodox experiment gone awry—an amalgam of disparate body parts drawn from a graveyard and fused into one by a mad scientist. And like that monster, it struck fear into the hearts of ordinary people everywhere. It had been cursed by the affliction of utter incompatibility, brought to bear by an uncompassionate, frightened, and uncaring world. It could never, and would never, be accepted, so it sat alone, greedily plotting its revenge on those it perceived as responsible for its eternal isolation—in this case, me, because I missed the school bus.

Negative space above the front bumper drew my eyes to where the grille once lived. It's as though it had removed itself from beneath the hood in protest—or out of a deep, abiding sense of respect—for its builder's own toothless grille. Two magazines sat on the flat black space beneath the rear window. *Peculiar*, I thought, knowing full well that Toothless Frank hadn't learned to read. Upon closer inspection, the mystery solved itself. They were porn mags. A copy of *Rustler* (a British knock-off of *Hustler*), and what I can only assume was a very rare, Asian-themed issue of *Juggs*. Both were proudly displayed, like jewelry against black velvet.

I had no beef with Toothless Frank. It was my own desperate situation that set me against him. Things were bad enough before he popped in a scratched-up eight-track cassette with a young Willie Nelson on the cover and spun the volume knob to the right. I've since learned to appreciate Mr. Nelson, but when I was a kid in Jersey, it felt like a violation. Over the unrelenting din of the treble-heavy acoustics, Toothless Frank yelled, "Betcha I can beat the buses!" an alliteration made all the more obscene by his toothlessness.

We never did beat the buses to school. Rather, we'd arrive precisely at the same moment the buses did. "Mamas, don't let your babies grow up to be cowboys," crackled Willie through makeshift speakers as our symphony of bad brakes and voluminous exhaust ground to a halt, coughing and wheezing, not thirty feet from the main entrance. I'd plead with Toothless Frank to drop me around back, behind the school.

"Please," I said, "please."

"Whatta ya mean? Why walk from the back?" he mumbled, oblivious to my nightmare.

I never was able to explain to him why I wanted to walk from the back. I couldn't say, "Well, Frank, do you see all my classmates' eyes basically falling out of their heads—through school bus windows, from behind classroom windows—and onto us and this environ-mental hazard you shamelessly call a car? Can't you see that behind those eyes are factories of judgment and prejudice? Can't you see them filling their coffers to the brim with crimson-colored hatred that will at some point be unloaded on anything that appears to be different from what they think they are? Can't you feel their faces curled into expressions that want nothing but the worst for me? Right now, they're all assuming that you're my father. I haven't seriously considered suicide yet, but you have the power to change that, and are doing so, by not allowing me to walk from the back."

Little did I know, a couple of decades later, I'd be forced to dance with children on the morning news.

16

CLEVELAND THE DRAGON

I'm listening to Big Mike, a raspy-voiced, narcissistic club owner / felon, explain to me why my expectation of a "full-room bonus" (extra pay based on good ticket sales) must have been an illusion. The ease with which he communicates this suggests that I'm not the first comedian he's had to convince. This guy wears lies like a suit. Everything he says is conveyed with a twitchy lack of eye contact. Ribbons of gray drift from our booth at IHOP as he chain-smokes his way through another pack of Pall Malls. He wears shades at breakfast.

We just finished morning radio, where Mike, perched over my shoulder like a cancerous parrot, called out bits of mine he'd like to hear on air. On the insult hierarchy, this lies just below "Dance, monkey, dance." Yet according to Mike, I'm "one a tha good ones" and he thinks "very highly" of me.

"I don't generally treat the talent to this kind of spread," he says, running the back of his hand over the edge of my plate of eggs. "You like my car?" he asks, referring to his new 911, a gleaming silver torpedo with a custom paint job and a large wing on the back.

"Yeah."

"It's the only one in Cleveland."

"It's the only Porsche?"

"With a wing like that."

"Yeah."

"Yup. Chicks like it."

"Yeah?"

"Yup . . . but then again, whatta they know? Been seein' this black stripper on the regular. She's one a tha good ones. I fucked some actresses out in Hollywood. I had some sweet ass." He laughs a laugh that's almost indecipherable from coughing.

And so it goes for another fifteen minutes, at which point I lie about having to make it back to my room for a conference call. As we exit the IHOP, Mike condescendingly points to a dwarf making his way onto a stool and cracks wise. In someone else's hands, it could have been funny, but this guy? I don't like mean humor. It's comedy's version of bullying. Hitting people who don't hit back should carry more severe penalties. I suspect his disposition is a result of years of self-loathing, or at least I tell myself that to make the ride with him back to the hotel more tolerable.

I hop in the passenger seat and watch Big Mike

contort his misshapen sixty-year-old frame into a car with the ground clearance of a skateboard. We inch out of the parking lot. Clearly he spent a hundred and twenty grand on this car to be noticed, not to drive it.

Once on the highway, he begins telling me about an idea he has for a movie based on his life. I'm staring out the window at a figure making its way on foot through the snow-blown landscape. Gloveless hands defend his face from the hard wind as cold, thick flakes dig like ticks into the folds of his jacket. Making little progress against the frostbite-inducing gales, the guy could be a statue, covered in frosting. Yet at this moment, I can't help but envy him for not being me.

"Bunch of scumbags in Hollywood," Big Mike says.

"Yeah."

"I mean, I hadda good time out there."

"Sounds it."

"Had some sweet ass. Lotta coke. Too much coke. Or not enough!" A cough/laugh. "This stuff just comes to me. You're a funny guy, though, I'll give ya that."

"Thanks."

"I used to do stand-up."

"Yeah?"

"Fuckin' audiences. They'll turn on ya. That's why I don't do relationships."

"Because of the audience?"

"Nah, they'll turn on you."

"Relationships?"

"What?"

"What?"

"Bitches."

We slide to a stop on a patch of ice in front of the hotel.

"If you wanna hang later, just lemme know," he says.

"That's okay, I have some writing to do."

"Should be some sweet ass in the club tonight."

"Have a good one."

Inhaling deeply, I swallow cold air as I shut the car door. It's as though I'd just surfaced from a deep dive. If only my hotel room were a hyperbaric chamber that I could sit in, gradually readjusting to normal, non–Big Mike atmospheric pressure.

Flopping onto the bed in my room, I attempt to sleep, but sleep doesn't come. I begin reading Alain de Botton's *The Consolations of Philosophy*, in which he discusses Seneca's ideas about unfairness being woven into the fabric of existence and how we must learn to suffer the inevitable with dignity and grace. If only Big Mike had read this before breakfast. If only I had read this before breakfast! Then again, if everyone were a philosopher, life would be a lot less funny. Nietzsche wasn't known for being a cutup. I guess the best we can hope for is balance—intellectual, emotional, psychological. If you're too heavy on any one of these, good luck.

17

CLEVELAND BACKSTAGE

That night I arrive at the club. Big Mike's drug-addled brother opens the door and asks me who I am for the fourth time in two days. I point to the six-foot poster of my face on the front wall for the fourth time in two days. Rolling his eyes as though I've disturbed him by showing up, he points in the direction of the greenroom. I walk through a black hallway filled with headshots of comedians. There's something sad about all these faces frozen in time, faces that stare out from beneath the glass, saying, "I'm here. Don't forget about me." Many of them are masked with expressions of happiness, but I know the truth.

I see Dom Irrera's face on the wall. Dom is a great comedian and a close friend. His picture makes me feel better about the world, less lonely, like seeing an old army buddy—someone you've shared trauma with, and laughter. His eyes understand the way I feel tonight. I laugh to myself about something he said to me last week. Apparently, Dom decided to go on a diet after discovering a slice of pizza in his pocket. I think about how funny something has to be for me to laugh out loud, alone, in a dark hallway. Then I open the green-room door and find Big Mike in a cloud of smoke.

"Hey! Good house tonight. I'll emcee."

"Great."

"Took this chick out to dinner. She eats like a horse." A laugh/cough, then he gets his breath back, a little triumph he celebrates with a deep pull on a Pall Mall.

"When you want the light?" he says.

"Forty is fine," I say, which means they'll flash a red light at me in forty minutes, at which point I've got another five minutes to wrap it up and get offstage. I have to be off at forty-five so they have time to turn the room over between shows: 250 people leave, 250 come in for the ten o'clock, if I'm lucky and we get a full house.

"Credits?" he asks me.

"Whatever."

"Whatta ya mean, 'whatever'? I don't believe in modesty. Gimme some credits."

"I don't care. *Tonight Show*, Comedy Central, Show-time, whatever."

"Some ass," he says.

"What?"

"Some ass."

"You like my ass?"

"No, my date!" Long laugh/cough. "I bang her Wednesdays and Fridays. She's one a tha good ones."

Lucky girl, I think.

At this point, Big Mike's brother cuts off the room's background music and turns down the lights. I can hear his voice over the PA system. "Thank you for coming out and supporting live comedy. Your headliner is in the back. How about a big hand for Don Davenon!"

For the third time in two days, he's gotten my name wrong. He's a thirty-year-old with Alzheimer's. I find him, like much of the world, simultaneously infuriating and hilarious.

"And how about a warm welcome for your emcee, Big Mike!"

The human smoke machine hits the stage and assaults the crowd with his first joke. It's a joke I've heard before, which means he stole it. Not only did he steal it, he didn't get it right. This guy turns funny into awkward at the speed of light. After fifteen minutes, I peek out from behind the curtain and see a roomful of people, befuddled as though they'd all been touched inappropriately, and more than once. Their expressions vacillate between dismay and despair.

"All right, folks, that's my time," says Big Mike, peering out from behind mirrored sunglasses. A smattering of applause can be heard. You can tell when people are applauding someone's departure as opposed to their performance.

People ask me if I get nervous before I go onstage.

The answer is not really. Performing stand-up on a television talk show can be a little unnerving because it's inorganic and brief, but the stage feels pretty natural. Whatever I feel is probably closer to adrenaline than nerves. Sometimes it feels almost comfortable, normal. Early on, I developed a strong tolerance for performance-related anxiety. Trying to get stage time for the first couple of years is a little like making it through hell week before you become a Navy SEAL. It's a soul-crushing obstacle course of sleepless nights and insecurity. So I've developed some mettle knowing it will never be as bad as it was. There were several months where, on Tuesdays and Fridays, I changed my last name to increase the likelihood that I'd receive stage time. It was a show run by the custodian of New York's worst comedy club (the bathroom overflowed twice a week, and there were holes in the wheelchair ramp). The show took place in what was basically a hallway. The owner of the club would allow stage time to anyone willing to work without pay. In this case, the building's super was given a whole show. The owner's only requirement to perform was that you be Puerto Rican like he was. I was allotted seven minutes at 1:00 A.M. Half the crowd was already drunk. I would swallow deep with humiliation but also laughter as I took the stage as Dov Dominguez.

18

CLEVELAND ONSTAGE

"Are you ready for your headliner?" bellows Big Mike.

The audience has flatlined. I feel like an ER doctor about to grab a defibrillator, knowing the patient's on his way out and will have to be shocked into regaining a pulse. "You've seen him on . . ."—blah, blah, blah—"For my money, he's one of the best guys working today." I can't help but smile, not because I don't think it's in the neighborhood of true but because he would probably use that line in his own credits as well. "Dov Davidoff!"

Stepping out from behind the curtain, I shake the degenerate's hand. "Keep it going for 'Sunglasses at Night,' everyone."

I can hear people talking among themselves. They're not settled yet. A good emcee will make certain the room's audience is focused before introducing the next act, let alone the headliner. Big Mike is not that guy. Standing still, I stare into the crowd, shielding my eyes from the spotlights so I can make actual eye contact with individuals. This draws people in. They're not sure what's happening. People are not enjoying themselves yet, but they're curious enough about my behavior to quiet down.

"What's your name?" I say to a muscular guy seated near the stage who's blatantly talking to the people at his table. I say it in a way that's both confrontational and playful. If done wrong, you can end up in an argument or a fistfight. If done right, it further focuses the room, creating an environment conducive to live comedy.

The show goes very well. I get a standing ovation from Mr. Muscles and the rest of his table. I really wish I could enjoy this part more. I think about how little time I have before the next show. I look down at the back of my right hand where I'd written some new material. I did half of it but kick myself about the half I didn't do. I'm happy everyone seemed to like the show. I think about how appreciative I am to have stand-up comedy compared to the rest of the entertainment business. I think about how little control I have over whether or not a television pilot works out. The collaborative nature of much of this business means that big projects often require a great deal of luck. With stand-up, I have some control. Not complete autonomy but some. I think about projects that I've missed out on because I wasn't well known enough or because the network executive wouldn't know funny if it crawled up his pant leg. It's the bittersweet feeling of a certain type of success. The kind that feels better than nothing, but, sadly, heightens your awareness of not *really* fulfilling your potential. I think about my father, who was never happy and died of AIDS much too young. I think about how funny he was. I think about how difficult his life was. I think about how much less difficult mine has been because of him. I feel guilty. I feel lucky. I feel ridiculous and self-indulgent for having so many feelings. I feel like I don't want to feel anymore tonight.

19

CLEVELAND
ONE SHOW DOWN,
ONE TO GO

After the set, I walk out to the bar and order a Stoli on the rocks. Right before I take a sip, this girl walks up and asks me to take a picture with her. I put the drink down and wait awkwardly while she yells to her boyfriend, "Ricky, take the fuckin' picture!"

Demure, I think. Judging from the way Ricky's face wrinkles up in confusion while staring at the camera, either he's drunk or he owns a time machine and has recently arrived here from the seventeenth century.

"So you're on TV, right?" he says.

"Yeah, sometimes," I say, but I want to say I've never understood pop culture or the place it has in some people's lives. I didn't grow up with much TV, so I guess I'm a bit immune to its aura.

I want to sit down and drink my drink but can't because I'm posing with this girl, and she's nice. My smile is getting more difficult to fake as her boyfriend fumbles with the camera. At this point, I'm wondering if he has actual neurological issues. Finally, he figures it out. "Ready?" he says. "One, two, three . . ." and nothing. The flash doesn't go off. He begins randomly tapping at the buttons. Eureka. He finally takes the pic. I watch them walk out, and I take a sip of my drink. The vodka is cold. It's both good and bad at the same time. It's good because it makes this environment a little easier for me to be a part of, and it's bad for the same reason. I pose for a few more pictures with people and make some small talk. I don't like small talk, but I've been alone most of the day, and it's better than nothing. I struggle with the idea that I need other people, but like the rest of the human race, I do. I have another drink, which makes the small talk easier. It also makes Big Mike, and his brother, and this city, more bearable.

I order another drink while making eye contact with a girl seated on the other side of the bar. Reflexively, I begin assessing the probability of her having come here single and alone. I don't see a drink on either side of her, suggesting she's not there with her boyfriend. Maybe she's waiting on someone. Judging from the length and tone of our eye contact, I'm willing to bet she's alone, or else she's willing to be. She's a blonde with big fake tits and an Ed Hardy hat. Everything about her says we have nothing in common. Under different circumstances,

I'd run in the other direction, but these are not those circumstances. I'm on the road. I'm gone in two days and won't be back for another year. She knows that. She's looking right at me and begins walking in my direction. I smile. She smiles back. She throws her arms in the air as if she's going to hug me. I think, *Wow, this chick isn't playing around*, as she steps to my left and throws her arms around a guy in a hat just like hers. Damn. My bad. I guess I'll have to go hit on someone else. But then—uh-oh, I smell smoke.

"There he is! Whatta ya drinkin'?" Big Mike says. Without waiting for a response, he looks up at the ESPN broadcast on the TV above the bar.

"Stoli, rocks—" I say.

"If only these pussies could cover the spread!" He cuts me off. He's got money on the game and doesn't care about my answer anyway. "Take a look at the rack on that one," he says, nodding in the blonde's direction. "Hey, you gotta light on ya?"

I shake my head, realizing that this guy doesn't always need a lighter, because he often lights the next cigarette off the one he's finishing. A lot of people throw around the term *chain-smoker*. This guy is the real deal. I find him entertaining in the way that all socially inept, self-hating sociopaths are—that is, until someone gets hurt, and then they're no longer entertaining. "Seating for the second show about to begin!" screeches the PA system. Smoky and me head back to the green-room through the black hallway of frozen faces.

20

CLEVELAND
THE SECOND SHOW

The second show goes a lot like the first. Big Mike, audience sadness, I defibrillate, the patient comes back to life. There's a difference between the early show and the later one. Eight o'clock shows are a little older, with a higher percentage of couples, yuppies, and families. The later shows are often younger and tend to be more vocal. This can be both good and bad. I'd prefer the energy of a later crowd but without the intoxication. Drinking can be great for comedy; like anonymity, it tends to loosen people up. The problems start when drinking becomes drunk. Drunk people don't appreciate subtlety. They're loud and stupid, like expensive clothing with big labels embroidered in the most visible places. I like to interact with the audience. I like to ask people what they'd like to talk about. I'm genuinely interested. It's also more engaging for me to work this way. Total spontaneity can be a liability, because you want to be funny, but you can't control what the audience will do or say. Many comics prefer to work in a more scripted way, like an actor in a play. It's a matter of taste, but if I had to do the same act in the same order every night, it wouldn't be long before I'd stop writing jokes and start writing a suicide note. When people have had a drink or two, they're more likely to talk to me. When people have had five or six, they turn into an alcoholic parent. You never know what will set them off. "*I thought you loved me.*"

Onstage, alcohol is a mixed bag, but when I'm offstage, it increases the probability of a one-night stand exponentially. Since losing my virginity all those years ago, I've been trying, unsuccessfully, to find some sexual balance. Even the night I met my first long-term girlfriend ended in a threesome. Her name was Rose. She was a model turned college student. She was standing outside of a comedy club with her girlfriend when I introduced myself. One drink led to another, and twelve hours later, the three of us found ourselves at a café in the East Village having breakfast. I spent the next four and a half years of my life with Rose. I loved her very much but couldn't figure out how to turn those feelings into the kind of commitment she required. In short, I was a fuckup. I regret my behavior and the way it made us both feel. Though years have passed, recalling the expression on her face when she realized we wouldn't be able to work it out fills me with sadness and not a little self-hatred. I revisit those feelings because I don't want to repeat my previous mistakes and lose someone I care deeply about, and in the process lose myself.

Monogamy has always been very difficult for me. Not naturally difficult, like any male mammal with red blood running through his veins. Difficult like almost impossible. Difficult like "I want to be in a committed relationship and experience deep, sustainable closeness and emotional resonance but can't because I have the sex drive of a rabbit eating carrot-flavored Cialis." Of course, this isn't just about drive. I would imagine a healthy drive could be harnessed and used to pull the cart of my sexuality in a productive, life-affirming, monogamous direction. What I'm describing is probably less about sexuality and more about filling some psychological void. A psychiatrist once made the observation that I didn't think I had an inherent right to live. He suggested that my need to justify my own existence could be leading me astray. Perhaps, but the problem right now is that the ten o'clock show just ended, making it almost midnight. I'm surrounded by the nubile, intoxicated, and misinformed.

21

CLEVELAND
ANOTHER DRINK

I order another drink, knowing I shouldn't. I just want to go back to my hotel and read or find something interesting on Netflix. Earlier, I'd begun watching *Cave of Forgotten Dreams*, a documentary by Werner Herzog about the oldest human-painted images ever found, forty-thousand-year-old paintings on a cave wall in France. I think about how inconceivably challenging life must have been forty thousand years ago. Then again, maybe difficulty is a state of mind. Maybe survival kept people so busy that they didn't have much time for contemplation. Existential considerations are a luxury paid for with free time and an abundance of food. I hear "Great show," and turn to meet the voice. The bedazzled Ed Hardy hat with the blond hair smiles back at me.

"Thank you. Appreciate it," I say.

"What are you drinking?"

"Where's your date?"

"He's a douchebag. We broke up."

"Wow."

"Forget it. So what's your plan?"

"Not one for extended grief periods, are—"

"Extended what? Anyway, he wasn't really my boyfriend."

"Great, so you're free to get *heavily* involved with me," I say with a wink and a smile, an attempt at humor. "What's your name?"

"Amber."

"Hey, maybe we find somewhere more quiet and less bright."

Oh, Christ, I just caught a whiff of the acrid fumes that precede the dragon. It's Big Mike making a beeline in our direction. He's looking right at her but talking to me. "There he is!" I scan the room for an exit. Nothing.

"Nice hat," he says to the blonde. He actually means it. "Hey, whatta ya say we all getta drink?" he says without looking in my direction for even a moment.

"Sure." Amber blinks. "He was really funny," she says, pointing at me.

"One a tha good ones," Big Mike spits back, mesmerized by the firecrackers of light ricocheting off her hat. I can't help but laugh at his response, because it could have been about anyone or anything. At this point, I begin fighting with the better part of myself. How long can I spend between these two? I'm torn between the desire to get in her pants and the need to find out more about Upper Paleolithic cave paintings.

The paintings will have to wait. I batten down the hatches and prepare for the coming storm. "Stoli, on the rocks, please."

Big Mike suggests we head to a local strip club.

"Oh, I have friends that work there," Amber says.

"What a coincidence," spits Big Mike, wide-eyed and without irony, as if both of us didn't already assume she was either a stripper or at least a woman very familiar with that world.

"Let's all do a shot!" Big Mike bellows at the bartender. I had just learned his name. It was Batas. "Batas! Patrón times three!" hollers Big Mike from behind a spinning index finger.

"I don't drink tequila," I say. He isn't listening. The bartender turns, executing the command with dexterity and purpose, peeling the bottle off the shelf, shot glasses, salt, lime, fast.

"Batas, at service, how doing?" the bartender says in heavily accented English with a smile and a nod.

"We drink tequila like Americans, not that sake shit your people drink," mutters Big Mike. Batas smiles the smile of the embarrassed and powerless. He's had to endure too much of this, but he needs his job. I tilt my head in Big Mike's direction, almost playfully.

"Tequila is Mexican, not American, and sake is Japanese, which this guy is not."

"No shit?" he pops back, with a "who gives a fuck" look on his face, swallowing his shot like the bad guy in a cowboy movie. "'Nuther one," Big Mike says.

"Batas, where are you from?" I say.

"Filipino," he says, struggling to break up a block of ice with a pick in his left hand while pouring a drink with his right.

"No shit? Guy's been workin' for me three years. Always figured Thailand." A beat passes.

"They don't have sake there either," I say, with an edge. Amber's eyes follow our conversation like a house cat watching a Ping-Pong ball. I can feel Big Mike's ego insisting that he take offense. I can't help myself at this point. It took all the self-control I could muster to not follow it up with "You fuckin' idiot." If it means dynamiting my relationship with this club and whatever money it brings me, or even fighting this dude out on the sidewalk, it'd be okay with me. I'm not a tough guy, but sometimes I hate injustice more than I care about myself.

"All right, nuffuhdis joint," says Big Mike, gesturing toward the back door. "Let's hit the Rusty Rail." I assume he's referring to a strip club, not a combination of old metal and cocaine. Amber nods. For her, like me, being alone at this point is too much to bear. Neither one of us have the sense of self necessary to walk away.

"Let's do it," I say.

A little earlier, I could have gotten out of this, but to not go now would make an enemy out of Big Mike. He initiated the face-saving. I'll do my part. We file out behind him, like passenger cars following a coal-powered locomotive spewing carbon monoxide as the whistle announces its departure from the station. "Did you drive?" I say to Amber, not wanting to ride shotgun with the animal.

"No," she says.

"Don't worry about it; we'll take my car," Big Mike announces, hitting unlock on his key fob with exaggerated physicality. A shrill *beep* pierces the air. It's much louder than usual. I think about the peculiar expression that must have crossed the Porsche salesman's face when Big Mike asked him if they'd be able to "turn up the horn." I imagine the conversation going something like this:

"Ya know that beep, when I hit unlock on the key thing?"

"What?"

"The key thing. The lock buttons. I want it loud."

The salesman's attempt at comprehension causes his neck to tilt several degrees, like a German shepherd staring at a robot.

"You want it loud?"

"Louder."

"O-kay, I'm, uh, I'm sure we can work that out for you," he says, staring at his own reflection in the baboon's sunglasses.

In Big Mike's mind, a montage of young women in bikinis whiplash their necks to and fro in an effort to locate the louder-than-usual beeps emanating from an IHOP parking lot. For Big Mike, this is not a car; it's "spinner bait," and the louder the better. I laugh to myself, thinking about the unusual level of wear and tear sustained in and around the lock/unlock area of a Big Mike key fob as he beckons the dysfunctional and fatherless.

"Nice car," says Amber.

Case in point, I think.

Opening the passenger door, I'm reminded that this car barely fits two. We all shoehorn in. I don't really mind. She smells cheap but good. Better than the human version of a burned Pall Mall sitting to my left.

CLEVELAND
THE RUSTY RAIL

THE RUSTY RAIL, declares the partially lit sign.

Comedians and strippers keep similar hours. Like predators in search of an ever-shrinking food source, we're bound to run into one another. I've had sex with a number of strippers, even dated a few, though none seriously—I'm not that self-destructive. They were all dysfunctional, and wacky, and psychologically tangled. A few were legitimately crazy. Each and every one of them was kind and generous to me when they could be.

Big Mike taps his horn, sliding his window down halfway. With a grin, he nods at the big black doorman as if to say, "I'm here. You're welcome." The doorman nods back, reluctantly, as we pull directly into a handicap spot. Exiting the vehicle feels like a contortionist's warm-up routine, but we manage.

"You're not going to get a ticket?" I ask Big Mike,

gesturing in the direction of the large blue HANDICAP ONLY sign.

He points at his handicap plates. "Got friends at the DMV," he says, punctuating the answer with an aggressive squeeze of his key fob. *Beep!* Again, I'd be lying if I said I didn't get a kick out of this guy.

"Dontrel!" squeals Amber, wrapping her arms around the doorman as if they're soul mates who'd been separated at birth. "How have you been?" she asks without really caring.

"Cool," he responds, knowing she doesn't care. It's not that she doesn't want to care. It's that she's probably not sure how to.

"So good to see you!" A second faux hug ensues. They barely know each other. There's a lot of pseudo-friendship among night people. A lot of misplaced hugs and "so good to see you"s, and complicated handshakes that go on too long. Silent contracts drawn up by people wanting more out of others than they are able to provide themselves. Authentic connections are replaced by synthetic ones. The embrace is inversely proportional to the friendship. Daytime relationships are different. I would do anything for my brother, but can't remember the last time I hugged him. At night, it's the opposite. The hug *is* the friendship. It's over when you let go, so we end up hanging on a little too long.

Big Mike nods at the girl behind the register, circling the air above our heads with his hand. "With you?" she says, referring to Amber and me. She waves us in without having to pay the ten-dollar entrance fee. Big Mike shoots me a wink that says, "Don't worry about it. I know people." I would have paid ten entrance fees to not have been subjected to that wink.

I like shitty strip clubs. They look like what they are. I wish everything were like that. I know what this place is, and I know what to expect. This is how Congress should look. Like what it is: a shitty club where everything is for sale, occupied by people with varying degrees of morality.

The three of us sidle up to the stage. It's your typical setup: glossy oak planks, brass poles, burgundy lights, and a naked girl surrounded by expressionless male faces. The usual suspects, with the exception of a large disheveled man wearing a gold chain, seated across from us, eagerly painting the wood with singles. The girl looks at the money and manages a smile, but this guy creeps her out more than most. His face is twisted up like a hungry cartoon wolf. I've spent a good deal of time in dicey neighborhoods and can't help but scan any new environment for potential threats. Peripherally, I keep an eye on him. He's not dangerous, just dumb, drunk, sad, and lost. He's not a wolf. He's a cartoon wolf. I relax and settle in.

Amber waves at a girl who looks a lot like her. The girl waves back. They know each other, but not well. They're "friends." Big Mike yanks out three singles and tosses them onto the stage. Amber's friend removes her glittering top and ascends the pole. Her athleticism is evident. I'm quietly impressed. She's graceful. It's sad—who knows what she could have been. Whatever it was would have been better than this. The song comes to an end. I pull a five and some singles out of my pocket and leave it on the stage. She bends down and picks it up, smiling courteously. Amber pulls out a ten and slides it into her hand. "Great job, honey," she says. I watch one of the expressionless men not leave any money at all.

A heavy-metal guitar riff tears through the speakers as Amber's friend's replacement bounds onstage with the vigor of a mongoose. She attacks the pole as though she'd just found out that it was responsible for all of her bad decisions in life. Up she goes, spinning. Around and around she turns before coming to an abrupt halt. As she descends the pole much too quickly, her eyes pivot left and right as she struggles to regain her footing. Frazzled, she places both palms on her head. Amber and I share a "what the fuck" look as she bolts from the stage. I notice something on the back of Amber's hand. It's difficult to determine what it is because strip club lights don't actually illuminate anything. It's red. I look at my hand, more red. I look out on the stage . . . red spot. Then another, and another, and another. Red spots are everywhere. I touch the spot on my hand. It's wet . . . it's blood. Droplets of blood are everywhere. Weird. Deductive reasoning tells me the mongoose must have hit her head on the ceiling, pinwheeling the blood, creating the Jackson Pollock painting we now inhabit. I inform my friends of this realization.

"Yuck!" Amber says, wiping her hands with a cock-tail napkin. Big Mike does the same. A strange silence settles over us. Collectively, we wonder if she'll be okay. More silence. At worst, she'll need a few stitches. She'll be fine. It's a cut, not head trauma. Then, with a shrug, from behind mirrored shades, and with impec-cable timing, I hear the smoking dragon say, "The song ain't over yet." We can't help but laugh, all three of us at the same time. We feel bad, but not too bad not to laugh. It's funny. We laugh in the way that friends do. In this moment, no one is jockeying for position, or trying to get in someone's pants, or trying to prove something. We're sharing the experience of wiping a stripper's blood off the backs of our hands, and even off each other's hands when we miss a spot. In this moment, we're all exactly where we want to be, among friends.

This is my dog Stella. She's eating peanut butter.
(Courtesy of Jessica Davidoff)

Me in a velvet vest. *(Courtesy of the author's mother, Addie Davidoff)*

This is my high school graduation photo. I was thrown out my senior year for lighting a small explosive in a particularly echo-ey area of the school. I was then put on "home instruction." Legally, I wasn't allowed within one hundred yards of the school, but I was given the right to earn a diploma at home. The principal said I could pick up my diploma the day after everyone else graduated. This is my vice principal. I dressed for the occasion with a gold chain and no shirt. Horrendous. *(Courtesy of the author's mother, Addie Davidoff)*

Jess and I on our wedding day. *(Courtesy of the author's mother, Addie Davidoff)*

My brother Orion and I.
We were ratty children.
(Courtesy of the author's mother, Addie Davidoff)

My father and I. *(Courtesy of the author's mother, Addie Davidoff)*

As a fat twelve-year-old in India on Sai Baba's commune. Because of the way my mother cut my hair, one of the shopkeepers thought I was a girl. *(Courtesy of the author's mother, Addie Davidoff)*

This is my father standing in the junkyard I grew up in trying to get someone back to work. *(Courtesy of the author's mother, Addie Davidoff)*

My mother, brother, and I. *(Courtesy of Aunt Marlene)*

As a fat twelve-year-old in India on Sai Baba's commune. Because of the way my mother cut my hair, one of the shopkeepers thought I was a girl. *(Courtesy of the author's mother, Addie Davidoff)*

This is my father standing in the junkyard I grew up in trying to get someone back to work. *(Courtesy of the author's mother, Addie Davidoff)*

My mother, brother, and I. *(Courtesy of Aunt Marlene)*

HBO's *Crashing* series premiere press event at Gramercy Theater. From left: Artie Lange, me, Pete Holmes, Hannibal Buress, Judd Apatow. *(Courtesy of the author's mother, Addie Davidoff)*

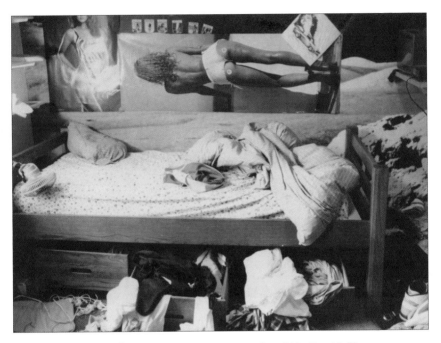

My bedroom as a kid. *(Courtesy of the author's mother, Addie Davidoff)*

23

MIAMI FUNNY

Palm trees sway with the breeze. Peering through a half-open window in the back seat of a pink taxi, I see olive skin and tight jeans dot sidewalks as wet, saline air clings to my skin. I'm excited because I'm supposed to meet up with my childhood best friend, Ricardo. He lives near here, or at least that's what the mutual friend that gave me his phone number told me. Not without some butterflies, I called him knowing that if our roles were reversed, he wouldn't have called me. I invited him to my show.

"Will you come?"

"Nigga, I'll be there." (*Nigga* is a term used by East Coast Puerto Ricans as well.)

I wonder if he'll think I was funny.

A NOTE ABOUT FUNNY

I remember the first time I said something that made others laugh. It wasn't funny to me, just logical, and it illustrated why the gift of comedy is often the curse of something else. A comedian's sensibility—the ability to observe from the outside looking in, in a way that's occasionally perceived by others as funny—was also part of what prevented me from connecting with classmates, who didn't appreciate the outsider among them.

It was in the sixth grade when our teacher asked us a question meant to inform our nascent ideas of morality. Through the gunsights of his eyes, he said to me, "For instance, if someone was to drop their wallet at a gas station, what would you do?"

"Depends what kind of car they drove," I said.

"What?"

"If it was a Mercedes, I'd take out the money and drop the wallet with whoever worked there. If it was a car like yours, I'd give it back."

He was insulted, though I genuinely meant no offense. That's really what I would've done. I should've been more tactful, but I didn't know better. And because offense was taken, my response, which had merit, was never discussed. He taught us nothing about morality but about a kind of political correctness—that an answer like mine, no matter how honest, wasn't necessarily the right one. I didn't learn anything about morality, but the uncomfortable chuckles from my classmates created in me a sensation of warmth, though also discomfort: I didn't know why they were laughing.

I wasn't aware of a desire to be funny. Like tusks on a walrus, funny was there before I knew it or how to use it. From my father, I had inherited an innate sense of timing and an irreverent nature. In the eighth grade, being voted class clown came as a surprise. I wanted to be a tough guy, an ambition that was nearly set straight when I had my jaw broken in two places in a street fight and when I narrowly escaped indictment for assault and battery with a deadly weapon. More on that later, but suffice it to say that I was more interested in inspiring fear than laughter.

24

MIAMI FOOTBALL CAMP

Prior to my freshman year in high school, desperate to fit in, I made the decision to attend football camp over the summer, even though I had never played. I signed and sent in the application without reading it. When I arrived at the camp, I noticed that people seemed to move in groups of twenty. I hadn't realized that this was in fact a "team camp," where whole teams come to stay and practice. Having never played any team sport, let alone football, I was questioned by the coach, a three-hundred-pound minotaur in compressed blue shorts—a guy who I imagine was raised in a wood-paneled basement on chicken wings and ESPN—about the whereabouts of my uniform and the rest of my team. Realizing I had neither, he allowed me to remain. I would have to sleep alone in a separate building, away from the team dormitories, and would be allowed to practice provided he could "find some pads or something."

Not knowing any plays, and wearing a uniform that looked like it had been knitted from mildewed drink coasters, I took the field as number zero.

"Hut. Hut. Hike!"

A large boy in a shiny uniform with greedy, close-set eyes lowered his shoulder, meeting with my abdomen. Standing over me, hands on hips like a triumphant Viking, he asked, "Did your team abandon you? What uniform is that?"

"I don't have a team," I croaked.

That evening, alone, and in a room that penitentiary inmates would've considered depressing, I passed out with the light on and the door ajar. The coach, bellowing, "Lights out!" shoved his way into my room. I must have been in the middle of a stress dream or a REM-related suicide fantasy, because I was startled. Ever the kinetic soul, I leaped from my bed with the electricity of a thousand hummingbirds. Graceless desperation made Benihana knives of my hands, dicing the coach about the neck, head, and face.

I suddenly became aware of what I had done. "Sorry, I didn't realize . . . I guess I was . . ."

"It's okay," he said.

And he meant it. He understood my anxiety, and I appreciated his sensitivity.

With an idea of what it would feel like to be paroled from prison, I left camp and returned to the yard of junk that was my home. Summer wasn't over yet, and I was as determined as ever to turn over the proverbial leaf as I made my way into the ninth grade. In high school, I would become what in my mind I was always meant to be: calm, audacious. I would be cool.

25

MIAMI RICARDO

It was in the eighth grade that I'd first noticed *Ricardo*. He was sidestepping in a semicircle, opposite the cheap multicolored lockers in our public school hallway. Wearing a thin gold chain and Saucony sneakers, he was slap-boxing with another boy—a play fight of sorts, where the objective was to tap or slap the other in the face. They were like tiger cubs playfully pawing at one another, unconsciously honing skills they'd later use to destroy and defend.

I was on the cusp of cool, and, to borrow from hip-hop, real recognizes real. I thought Ricardo might be real. He would eventually become my partner in crime. As seniors, and much too cool for most of those around us, we would be voted "class inseparables," as we had become something of a two-man posse. Incidentally, my only other distinction in high school was that I would, as a senior, after already having been thrown out of school, be voted "teachers' terror," essentially a combination of "class clown" and "most likely to end up in prison."

Ricardo was a Puerto Rican transplant who had recently arrived from Spanish Harlem, and it was with him, starting at the age of fourteen, that I would learn to walk the kinds of New York City streets that most white boys never see. It was with Ricardo that I would learn to dance; he may argue it, but compared to the average white guy, I'm pretty light on my feet. At the Limelight or the Underground, we would skip, dip, and hop to whatever the DJ spun. It was on the floor of his bedroom the summer before high school that I would have my first sexual experience with a girl my age. And with him, I would procure a little blow from the Bronx, cut it with baby laxative, and resell it to people whose experience of the world was whiter than my own. It was with his aunt and uncle—in the hood, aunts and uncles are often much younger than they are elsewhere—that I would live from time to time. It was with him that I would learn to hold my eyes and my head at such an angle and in such a way as to say, "If you wanna fuck with me, you'd better be dangerous."

26

MIAMI CHUCKY

With this head of testosterone-fueled ambition, I was headed into high school, incautiously searching for that elusive jungle panther that is "cool." How, I wondered, could this exalted state be achieved in as little time as possible? I decided to approach my neighbor Chucky for advice on the subject.

Chucky was four years my senior at seventeen. He had just dropped out of high school to take a job in sanitation as a way to satisfy his all-consuming ambition to purchase a three-wheeled motorcycle before his eighteenth birthday.

Ambling over, looking suitably deferential, I stammered my question to him. "Any advice . . . ? About to go into high school. First year, ya know . . ."

Chucky took a deep breath before arching a leg onto the chrome front bumper of an old car that had exchanged its wheels for cinder blocks. His boot, and with it, his body and head, were reflected in the bumper in such a manner as to evoke Ichabod Crane. With wind-tousled black hair, Chucky, gazing off into the horizon, spoke one line: "Chicks like thin leather ties."

My first and last experience with beer also took place at the foot of this great thinker. Chucky, ever the forebear of Socrates and Plato, suggested we "slam some beers," but not before inhaling some especially toxic marijuana—Skunk Bud, if memory serves. Chucky whooped around our patch of dirt like a yellow-crowned night heron in search of a mate. He encouraged me to guzzle five or so cans of a beer so awful that even craven alcoholics would have had to run out of mouthwash before considering it. My body suddenly desired nothing more than a separation from itself. I began projectile vomiting.

Afterward, delirious, I trespassed across several of my neighbors' scruffy mini-lawns to the home of the object of my desire, Nicole, a girl of about fifteen with unusually large breasts, who I was certain would return my affection. Chucky followed. The home was dark, its occupants—six sisters and two parents—were sleeping. My legs trembled as I began crowing upward in the direction of Nicole's second-floor window, cheered on by my deranged flightless bird of a neighbor. Not only did she not return my sentiment, but after hearing me holler, *"Show me your tits!"* for the seventh time, a deep, resonant male voice began issuing ulti-matums, on the order of "Leave, or I'll kill you."

I think about how Ricardo would've responded had he caught me, drunk, crowing up at the second floor of that house. He would've put a stop to it and told Chucky to get lost, but he wasn't there to save me from myself.

Early September sun burned bright on the morning of my first day in the ninth grade. Marching into my high school's main office with the confidence that can only come from wearing a black leather jacket, multi-zippered parachute pants, and a thin red leather tie, I changed my name to Steve. Putting the past behind me, I decided I would create a new, improved, invulnerable me. Like other formerly chubby kids, my body was evolving into something lean, hard, and sinewy. I needed a new identity to replace the one I was fleeing.

I never successfully became Steve. It never felt right, and whenever the name was mentioned, I looked around for the person being called, thinking it odd that no one answered. I settled back into Dov, only now with the faux confidence of a guy named Steve wearing a leather tie.

27

MIAMI
GRAND THEFT AUTO

Outside of high school, my attempts to harness my inner cool found other outlets. I never really devoted myself to my fledgling marijuana and cocaine import-export operation, so I worked from time to time on weekends. I loaded, unloaded, and sold discount athletic clothing at a local outdoor flea market under the auspices of Joe, an angry, cheap human pumpkin with sideburns. After one particularly long, frigid day, and already something of a budding moral relativist, I decided to "borrow" an order form from my boss, the jack-o'-lantern. This form had pricing and contact information for Russell Athletic Irregulars, the very same company from which he purchased his discounted irregulars for resale, with respectable profit margins. My father, eternally interested in anything meant to be concealed from the IRS—whom he perceived as none other than the embodiment of evil on earth—agreed to lend me two thousand dollars. With this, I would order one thousand pounds of Russell Athletic Irregulars. A couple of months later, I repaid my father. I was still fourteen, still loading, unloading, and selling discounted/irregular athletic clothing, but now I had a couple grand in my pocket to show for it.

Flush with cash, and in search of new sources of excitement, I decided to steal a car. It was actually my friend's idea, but it sounded perfectly reasonable to me. This would be the first and last time I ever stole a car. Accompanied by Fergus, a wild-eyed, ungainly Irishman, I lay in wait behind the soot-covered bushes of a convenience store parking lot. We were like two fifteen-year-old hyenas, salivating in expectation. The time to strike had arrived. We aimed ourselves in the direction of our luckless victim. This man had the misfortune of having hastily left his keys in the ignition as he ran into the store for a Slurpee or a bag of mixed nuts. Or perhaps, ironically, he was hoping to get lucky with a lotto ticket.

Fergus charged and dove into the driver's seat. Tearing over the hood and into the passenger seat like a TV cop, I yelled, "*Go!*"

Fergus's pupils were quarters and still expanding. For a moment he couldn't speak. The pressure of the situation along with his inherent unsteadiness had twisted the expression on his face into that of a panicked owl. Finally, in a burst of sound, he shouted, "I can't drive stick, man!" I'd managed to partner with the only wannabe car thief in Jersey that couldn't operate a manual transmission.

Like two bumbling idiots in an old-time comedy, we managed to switch places without exiting the vehicle. Peeling out of the parking lot and racing into the moonless night, we shrieked like hyenas neck deep in zebra blood. This adrenaline was a kind of sustenance that would allow us to make it through another week before the boredom drove us back together in search of something destructive. On a back road, we rendered the vehicle undriveable, as its flimsy, wishbone suspension met with more gravity than it could handle. And like the hyenas we were, the sounds we made continued through the night, long after the car cut out. To the untrained ear, our high-pitched celebration may have rung of revelry, even joy. But often that's what crying on the inside sounds like.

My life could've gone irreparably sideways on any number of evenings. The fever of youth slamming headlong into the repercussions of adulthood never makes a pretty sound.

28

MIAMI
EARLY RELEASE

It was around this point in my life, as a sixteen-year-old sophomore in high school, that I would be granted "early release." This was a program initially created for seniors with after-school jobs who had completed all their necessary course work and were bound for college. For me, it was because I had been thrown out of a few afternoon classes. Shortly after my algebra teacher called my mother with the news that I was "the worst behaved student he'd had in ten years," I was thrown out of that class. Subsequent dismissals arrived that month—one for, among other things, outfitting our science classroom door handle with a fetal pig head. The final straw in English class was when I'd been caught fingering the girl next to me while our teacher read aloud to the class from a short story written by a Holocaust survivor.

Early release meant leaving school every day by noon. This provided me with extra time to find new and different means of self-destruction. Not wanting to be held back in the tenth grade, I was forced to attend summer school. Interminably late, I often appeared in a bathrobe, the pockets of which were filled with candy and under which I'd smuggled a small pillow for napping.

It was around this time that my father had remarried and moved away from the house I'd been living in since I was born. My mother left too. She asked that my brother and I come live with her, but I had no interest in choosing between parents and so decided to stay put. My father owned the house, and such was his hatred for my mother the he was happy to forgo rental income provided that I didn't move in with "that woman." Knowing it was illegal for anyone under the age of eighteen to live alone, my father evaded child protection laws by persuading a twenty-year-old family friend to act as my legal guardian. This arrangement ended abruptly. My guardian stumbled upon a one-eighth-pound sack of marijuana hidden in my closet and moved out for fear of arrest. My father knew better than to attempt reform, so, after asking me what I had paid for the sinsemilla and if I could get my money back, he allowed me to stay long after my guardian headed for the hills.

Though I was clearly approaching dangerous speeds on the autobahn to nowhere, being a degenerate had its upside. By this time, I had become rather popular with a certain segment of my town. I had a number of friends, and girls, all of whom belonged to the base-born class of which I was a member. The upside, however limited, was that I did what I wanted, and a lot of it, and so did my friends and girlfriends. The kinds of girls who made themselves available to guys like me often hail from broken families like mine. Sex for them, and for me, was likely a way to fill parts of themselves not satisfied through healthier means. They, like me, didn't live with an eye on tomorrow, because a real tomorrow means examining your life today. Self-awareness tends to require hope, and hope requires faith in the possibility of something better.

I've had sex with hundreds of women, maybe as many as a thousand. No way to know. I'm not bragging. In fact, any pride I experience is more closely related to the pride one feels after having taken revenge. I mean a universal revenge, directed outward, but inevitably reflected inward. The revenge of taking something back from a world that I wish would have provided me with more love and compassion. The revenge of promiscuity—or, for that matter, of getting laughter—is seeking out a replacement for what you never felt in the first place: acceptance. The acceptance I wanted, but didn't get, resulted in a hostile relationship with a world that I didn't really see myself as a part of.

A showbiz agent, describing what he looks for in potential male acting clients, once said to me, "I like to rep guys like you, ya know. You're the kind of guy girls wanna fuck and guys wanna hang out with, like a movie star." Having paid the unrecoverable price of a childhood spent in dark spaces, I had been rewarded with virility, means, and access. The juvenile fantasy had come true, but fantasies should come with a disclaimer, because like so much of life, imagination and reality make strange bedfellows.

29

MIAMI BOOM!

I want to experience a monogamous relationship. I crave stability. I don't want to chase the tail of my sixteen-year-old fantasy through adulthood, never having known intimacy. If monogamy isn't possible, I want to arrive at that decision as the result of considered effort, not a defensive acceptance of defeat because the idea of that kind of closeness seems too substantial for me, too foreign, or too scary. Monogamy is unnatural, undeniably. That doesn't mean it isn't preferable. I like to think that part of an actualized existence involves finding the least of all evils, of acknowledging that the ideal doesn't exist. "Do the best you can with what you have." It sounds simple, but it's challenging in practice. And to develop an idea of what our "best" means, we must stare into the painful abyss with steely nerves, with the resolve of someone with more strength than I have yet to exhibit. But I will not be denied, because I won't give up.

By the way, it's exasperating when someone behaves in the ways that I have, then in prime, politically correct fashion, acts as though little pleasure was taken, as if it were all foisted upon them by an unjust universe. They're lying. There are those parts of my life that aren't dignified or life-affirming, or who I want to be. They may be masking an inner life associated with sadness. But there's no denying that they are the source of many smiles and much laughter.

My high school years came to an end in a series of explosive moments. First literally, as I lit and tossed an M-80 (a small explosive, roughly the size of a shot glass) at the high school's main office, which housed the student administration staff, the vice principal, and the principal. Why I did this remains a mystery. I like to imagine that this was my attempt to divide time, to create a before and an after. I needed something—some sound, some reaction, a sort of seventh-inning stretch—before ending the four-year exercise in monotony that was my high school education.

The next day, while I was eating breakfast with my mother, she said, "Oh, by the way, you know Sean"—a female gym teacher friend of hers—"well, we've been dating."

Oh, I thought, *would you mind if I finish my eggs before we get to your newfound lesbianism?* I guess for someone else this may have struck them as a big deal, but my mother has often defied explanation. I added this fact to the pile. *Whatever works*, I thought.

Later the same day, I was called into the principal's office. Apparently, an eyewitness and budding Good Samaritan dropped a dime on me. The principal explained to me that aside from having been "frightened to death" himself, one of his teachers had to be taken to the ear doctor. He let me know that I would never enter this building again; I had been written up for disciplinary incidents well over a hundred times, and to remain under his roof represented a "real and present danger." I was told that if I were seen within several hundred yards of the school, the police would be called and I would be arrested for trespassing, in addition to which a restraining order would be filed. He let me know that if I was to "play by the rules," I would be placed on "home instruction"—a program in which teachers from the school would be made to stop by my house, drop off schoolwork, then stop by again to retrieve it. Essentially, I would be given a diploma. They wanted me out.

And so, unburdened by the need to attend a school, at seventeen, Ricardo and I would move to the Lower East Side of Manhattan. I knew that I would never again return to the place where I grew up.

———

"Twenty-two fifty."

"What?"

"We're here, at the club," says the man driving me through Miami. "You owe me twenty-two fifty . . ."

Snapping back into the present, I feed a twenty and a ten to the dark, outstretched hand. His fingers feel like an intrusion. They're tentacles of reality, piercing the cocoon of my memory.

"Sorry. Lost track."

Exiting the taxi, I spot my childhood best friend. After years of distance, a memory manifests itself in front of me in physical form. Ricardo stands alone, feet apart, alert, face half-lit by the noirish glare of street-lights. The flicker of a cigarette lighter break-dances across his face before settling on the joint between his lips.

My stomach tightens around a mini-flood of emotions, but my training insists that they move no higher. My face is no snitch.

"Yo, Rick."

A snake of marijuana smoke slithers in my direction. Ricardo nods. His face is no snitch either. This is the guy who made me feel less alone, when alone was all I knew.

"What up, nigga?"

"What up, man?"

His wrist turns the joint up and outward, as if to say, *Wanna hit?*

"Nah, I'm cool. Maybe later."

Ricardo pulls deep on the joint, exhaling more loudly this time. An image of Toothless Frank appears in my mind, the way he'd feed a four-foot stretch of garden hose into the gas tank of a car. He would siphon by inhaling fast and hard, then quickly removing the hose from his mouth.

There is something about city streets at night that both muffle and compound the sounds of humanity. Ricardo and I walk wordlessly in the direction of the club. What we lack in language we communicate with movement. I can't help but wonder what we've lost to become who we are: calm, audacious.

30

SAN ANTONIO
THE ALAMO

It's summertime in San Antonio. The air is hot and wet like it's about to rain, but it doesn't. I'm lonely, and I haven't slept well. The club is a fifteen-minute drive from downtown where I'm staying. I don't want to go there. I didn't want to come here. I feel stuck. I feel like the air, uncomfortably anticipating the relief of a rain that never comes. I just want this gig to be over with. I want to go home. I want to feel like I have a home, but I don't. I want to feel like I have something that makes me feel at home. I don't even know what a home is. Even my depression is filtered through my ADD; my head bounces from the idea of going home to not having a "home" to wondering what a home is, then being angry with myself for feeling self-pity.

I feel the weight of my singlehood, of not being in a relationship with a woman I can share my feelings with.

I feel the weight of myself. I feel myself getting older. I feel the weight of my past and my future, and my present. My life is easier than so many other people's lives, but of course the kind of comfort this notion offers is of the cold variety.

It's 7:00 P.M. The phone in my hotel room rings. My ride is here. He works at the club, and he's a nice enough guy, but I don't want to talk. He does. I oblige, but after a bit of banter, I say, "Excuse me," and pretend that my phone needs me. I tap at the screen, hoping this guy doesn't bring up baseball or the weather or some other subject that'll make me want to leap out of a moving car.

We arrive at the club. It's next to a movie theater. On my way up the escalator, I look at the posters lining the wall. The coming attractions could hardly be less attractive. For a moment, I feel jealous of one of the actors on the poster. I'd rather be on a film set than having to do this show tonight. Then I think about how boring film sets can be. There is no reprieve from my mood tonight. I don't want to do stand-up. I don't want to be in a movie. I don't want to be home, wherever that is. Essentially, there is no place I want to be right now. If you had told me there was an attractive woman waiting in the manager's office for me and that she'd like to perform fellatio on me, but not before handing me a compliment and a gift, I'd shrug and say, "Thanks, but it's not a good time."

I'm standing in the showroom now. It's a good

house, meaning the club is almost full. The emcee calls out my name. I jump onstage, and not five minutes into my set, some guy in the front row starts in. I don't even remember what he said, but it was humorless. It was said in a way that made me not want to respond. I generally engage the hecklers so as to let them know who's in control. I let them know this will not go well for them. This is one of those hecklers who won't get it. He won't understand that it's not worth it. He's drunk and angry looking and sitting with two friends just as drunk as he is. I ignore him, hoping he'll go away. "That's a good one!" he bellows after a joke. What he means is that he saw other people laughing, but since he's not really here to listen, he wants me to acknowledge his presence. I smile and nod as I slide into another joke. Like a scene out of a karate movie, where the bad guy is cartoonishly bad, this idiot begins toasting with his buddies. The three of them clink beer bottles. Most of the room hears them. I can no longer pretend that they aren't there. "Quiet down," I say. I'm not going to attempt to engage these guys, perhaps incite some self-awareness. Like I said, these aren't those guys. I just have to move on with the show, but organically, so I take a pause and shrug, guess it's just one of those nights.

Clink.

Another toast rings through the air. I look over at them again. They look up at me. Only this time, I see the faces of the four people seated behind the Clink

Brothers. Two of those faces belong to these big blond guys whose expressions indicate their disdain for the hecklers. They're seated with two gals, and I can see they feel insulted for me.

Another clink rings through the air as their beer bottles make contact for the last time. I've had enough. "Can you shut the hell up?" I say to the ringleader, walking closer to his table, hoping they'll see the light. They don't.

"Relax yourself," the ringleader says.

"What!" I say, standing about three feet from him.

"Just be funny," he says.

I've had it. "Fuck you," I say.

He pops up like he's going to come at me. He's drunk. I react first and push him backward over a chair. His two friends jump up. I'm in trouble.

As if on cue, one of the blond guys stands up, takes his shirt off, and yells, "He told you to shut the fuck up!" The second blond guy stands up too, and it's on. His left hook lands as the first Clink guy goes down. The other blond guy throws a right hand. Down goes another Clink guy. The ringleader pops back up just in time to have his own head get bounced off the metal handicap railing. Security runs in to break up the melee. The Clink Brothers absorb another five or six shots apiece.

I didn't think anything could put me in a good mood that night. I was wrong. Nothing makes me happier than justice, in this case, Texas-style. Had this incident happened in most places, the Clink Brothers would've gotten away with their offense. Had this happened in San Francisco, I would've heard a bunch of "Dude, that's not cool." But we're in Texas right now. There's a lot I don't like about Texas—I don't like the heat, I'm generally not a fan of their politics. But I love these two blond guys right now, and I love their brand of justice. You can preach all you want about nonviolence, and much of the time you'd be right. To me, this is not one of those times. You could've said, "Dude, that's not cool," a hundred times to the Clink Brothers, but you may as well have been talking to the wall.

Nah, that night was a special night. On that night, in that moment, the order of things was just as it should be. Everything made sense.

The lights come up in the showroom. The owner's voice comes out over the PA system. "Everybody out."

Why? I think. *Let's continue with the show.* I hop back up onstage, grab the mic, and say, "Hey, let's continue; everybody relax."

"It's my club, and I want everybody out!" hollers the owner through PA system.

I jog off the stage and into the back of the room, where the owner sits behind glass in the DJ booth. I assure him that there is no need to cancel the show. The Clink Brothers have been dealt with, they are gone, and there are a lot of perfectly decent people here. People that paid good money, got babysitters, drove through traffic, parked the car, and walked into this club.

They should be entertained. After a bit of back and forth, he acquiesces, dims the lights, and announces that the show would continue.

I walk back onstage, and for the first several minutes there are no laughs. I realize that the laughs won't come until people calm down, so I try to acknowledge what had just happened in a way that will break the tension. I point at the Clink Brothers' table and say, "Brought to you by Budweiser."

I hear the first laugh, then two, then five, then most of the room. Before you know it, we are all back on track. It was one of the most satisfying shows I've ever had.

Afterward, I meet up with the blond guys and buy them a drink. We stand outside, sipping vodka. The air is still warm but a little cooler, and moving. "What a dick," one of the blond guys says.

"You wonder what people are thinking," I say. After an awkward pause, I add, "So you guys live around here?"

"Yeah," they say.

"Good lookin' out," I say, picking my glass up to meet theirs.

"Yup," they say.

I'm grateful for these two guys. We don't have much to say to one another—we don't even talk about the fight. We're too old for that. Also, I get the sense that kickin' ass on a Saturday night isn't that uncommon for these two.

I spot my ride back to the hotel at the bottom of the stairwell. I initiate the touching of glasses again as I make my exit. "Again, good lookin' out, guys. You are appreciated."

"You too," one of them says with a nod.

I put my drink down and head for the stairs. I don't know who coined the phrase *Don't mess with Texas*, but they weren't wrong. San Francisco is great, but thank God I'm in San Antonio tonight.

31

SAN ANTONIO TOUGH

As a kid, I remember wanting to be a tough guy. Because I grew up feeling awkward and defenseless, tough made sense to me. But what is tough? I guess tough was connected to self-esteem in my mind. It meant standing my ground, even if I didn't want to. It meant that I'd made the decision to fight, even if the outcome didn't seem favorable. Because to do otherwise could mean losing everything.

I walked away from an altercation when I was twelve or thirteen, where some other kid had become aggressive with me. I remember feeling fear. The kid looked scary: black jacket, bad haircut, dirty shoes. Nothing says *I don't care* like a kid with dirty shoes. He said something to me—I forget what it was, but it felt like a challenge. I remember responding with something along the lines of "I don't have a problem with you." I remember the smug look on the kid's face as he walked away, like he'd taken something from me. I felt like I'd swallowed a rock. It lasted for the rest of the day and into the next. The thought that he was walking around with something that was mine bothered me. That part of me was not for him. And since I felt like I had little else, it hurt that much more. I didn't have popularity. I didn't have good grades or athletics to hang my hat on. I didn't have self-esteem. I simply didn't have many parts, and so I couldn't afford to give any of the ones I had away.

Tough never ends well. Even tough guys don't really want to be tough guys. They want to be safe. They want to not be fucked with. They want to protect their loved ones. They want respect. They want all of that bad enough to become tough. Watch any interview with Mike Tyson; tears follow most questions surrounding his childhood. He gets choked up because the feelings of humiliation, insecurity, and fear are still so close to the surface. Thirty-five years later, he's crying about some kid having taken his lunch money. He's not tough: he's talented, and furious, and afraid. Combine those, add a trainer, some structure, and opportunity, and you have the makings of a great fighter.

Maybe there is no such thing as real toughness. Maybe toughness is just sunblock for the UV rays of fear. Tough is what you become if you don't have anything else to aspire to. I never became tough, not really. I became a little crazy and tough enough that if you were a bully, I wasn't the guy you'd choose to go after. Tough enough to convince people that I didn't care about the consequences of an altercation. Because I didn't; in those moments, I only cared about not feeling humiliated. If anyone was going to hurt me, it was going to be me.

32

SAN ANTONIO ASSAULT AND BATTERY WITH A DEADLY WEAPON

At eighteen, and cloaked in a lack of self-awareness bordering on delusion, I was arrested for assault with a deadly weapon. I was inside a store when my girlfriend looked through the window and saw a group gathering around her car. I peeked out and spotted six or seven guys. One of them was leaning against the driver's-side door. I stepped outside to take a look.

Feeling two arms wrap around me from behind was not what I was expecting. This was no friendly bear hug. It was the kind of hug that says you're not going anywhere. I quickly identified the greasy long-haired gentleman moving in my direction as the ringleader, an assumption I felt even more confident about when he punched me in the face.

What the fuck is going on? Knowing I didn't want to hang around and find out, I began twisting and turning in such a way that the guy holding me figured it was more trouble than it was worth. I broke free and began running, but I had just gotten out of a soft cast after an ankle injury and wasn't as fleet of foot as I would have been otherwise. Realizing I couldn't out-run the guys that were now following me, I felt for the knife I was carrying in my back pocket. I forget why I was carrying this knife. It could have been junkyard-work related or self-defense related. It wasn't some-thing I carried often. Slowing my pace, I pulled the knife, popped the blade, and turned to meet the pack. The long-haired ringleader stopped in front of me as the other dirtbags flanked me from the side and rear. Surrounded and frightened, I held the blade in front of whoever came closest. In this case, it was the guy who had just punched me in my face, the ringleader.

Wanting to impress his friends or just plain crazy, he stood in front of me, put his hands up, and said, "I love knives."

I hope his friends were impressed. I certainly was. He threw a punch. I ducked and lunged at his face with the blade. He missed. I didn't. His face opened up. For a moment, there was no blood. Then it came, lots of it. Time stood still for a beat. Fear flashed across the ringleader's face as the reality of what had just hap-pened set in. I heard someone yell, "Get the bat!" and one of his degenerate buddies leaped behind a bush. The ringleader's left hand felt for the blood pouring down his face and neck. For a brief moment, it was just me and him. Our eyes locked on each other, both of our brains grappling with what had just happened and what to do next.

I felt something slam into my right forearm as the knife flew out of my hand. Realizing one of his buddies had kicked me from behind, I spun and tried to run through a hole in the circle I was surrounded by, but there was nowhere to go. I heard the ringleader scream as he ran up behind me, swinging wildly at my head. I ducked again and threw a right hand, catching him on the open side of his face. My hand felt wet as blood painted my knuckles. His crew had just caught up to me as the wail of a police siren became audible. The cop car came closer, and they scattered.

I was under arrest, happily. I allowed myself to be cuffed, enthusiastically, and hopped into the back of that police car.

Several months later, I was brought before a grand jury for assault and battery with a deadly weapon. Grand juries are there to determine whether the state has enough to charge you officially. I was sure I was innocent on the grounds of self-defense, but my attorney cautioned me against overoptimism. The old saying is "A prosecutor can indict a ham sandwich"—meaning it doesn't take much to indict.

I had dressed in a way suggestive of a career in academia, including fake glasses and a tweed sport coat. Had the jury seen how I normally dressed, they might have taken me off the street for the sheer appearance of menace. My attorney impressed upon me the importance of communicating both the depth of fear I experienced and the regret that followed—and I did, though if I'm honest, I hadn't really been aware of much fear. I guess I was afraid. I just wasn't aware of it in the moment.

Maybe that's what real fear feels like, a paralysis of cognition—you're so afraid you can't feel anything but the need to survive. As far as regret, nope, none, didn't feel any of that. The guy that came after me was a bad guy. I'm sure he loved his mother, maybe even his dog. But he was a bad guy. I'm all about examining the complexities of human behavior in an attempt to understand ourselves, but sometimes you can't afford to care. When it's him or me, nonviolence isn't a realistic move in the playbook of life.

33

SAN ANTONIO
BROKEN JAW

The next and last time a physical altercation turned into something serious wasn't too long after the knife incident. I was walking around the Feast of San Gennaro in New York City with some guys I knew from Jersey. I'm not sure what happened, but suddenly the crew I was with was exchanging words with another crew just as dumb and misguided as we were.

Not wanting to be thought of as "less than," I approached one of the guys on their side. I said, "Is there a problem?" This is embarrassing for two reasons. One, it means I was an insecure idiot with a host of emotional issues. Two, it's hacky. I should've been able to come up with something more creative.

The guy said, "No, no problem," and when I

turned around, he hit me—hard. I wasn't knocked out, but I hit the ground. The guys I was with went after the guys he was with. Cops arrived almost immediately. One of my guys caught a flying bottle on the forehead. On the sidewalk, he lay still, his head surrounded by a half-moon of blood. I held my jaw; something didn't feel right. I couldn't close my mouth.

After what seemed like a whole day spent in the emergency room waiting area, I was told that my jaw had been broken in two places and that I'd need surgery. My jaw would have to be set, then wired shut for two months. After a month of liquid nourishment, chewable food felt like a fantasy. Walking into a supermarket or ordering off a menu began to feel like a pipe dream. One day I walked into a pizza shop and ordered a calzone with extra sauce. Ravenously, I hustled home and threw it in a blender. Like most decisions made through the haze of desperation, my calzone smoothie wasn't what I'd dreamed it would be. The expectation of happiness creates a lot of unhappiness, I thought.

My jaw was broken, but much to my girlfriend's chagrin, my interest in sex hadn't faded. She didn't really want to have sex with me because my mouth was wired shut, which prevented me from breathing normally where physical exertion was involved. A few minutes into lovemaking and I began to sound like

Darth Vader. I suggested that we do it dog-style. We tried, but that just made it worse; Darth Vader was now behind her.

I don't ever want a broken jaw again, not if I can help it. Sometimes life calls for toughness, but there's never a call for being a tough guy. Tough guy is a dead end. It's a psychological trap that can prevent you from experiencing yourself more honestly. Tough guys have trouble with intimacy and vulnerability like the rest of us, but they're not supposed to look at it or talk about it. They're too busy being tough.

I've spent enough time around tough guys in my life to learn a thing or two. Not prison-gang, murderer tough, but jailhouse, small-time-drug-dealer tough. I saw the way their eyes moved, and the way they didn't. Hanging out in the projects, you begin to realize that real tough guys aren't so tough. They're sensitive—sensitive enough to kill you, and sensitive enough to take what's yours because someone had once taken what was theirs. They're sensitive enough to never want to experience the pain of vulnerability again.

Tough may be a less-than-ideal option, but it's better than being a victim. Or so we might convince ourselves. Ultimately, we're all victims. We're victims of time, and of our minds, and age, and our families, and the circumstances we're born into.

We're all victims of something by the end, but if we live our lives as tough guys, then we'll become victims much sooner—victims of ourselves.

34

AMSTERDAM MUSHROOMS

Who hasn't eaten too many mushrooms in Amsterdam, then found himself lying on the floor of a taxi being yelled at in Dutch by the driver, all the while crying because he thought he was locked inside of a computer?

I think psychedelic drugs can be interesting, provided you don't take way too many before hopping into a cab in Europe. Seeing things from a new perspective is rarely regrettable, and you don't generally hear about psychedelics leading to violent or antisocial behavior. You never hear about the KKK dropping mescaline, then looking for someone to lynch. They'd likely become very involved with the rope, its unseen connection to the world beyond and the universe within.

No, it's liquor, not hallucinogens, that lends itself toward the lighting of crosses and the wearing of hoods.

It's always some angry drunk with a bottle of bourbon and some lighter fluid that makes trouble for decent folk. Whiskey fuels more bigotry in one week than all the acid ever taken. No one has ever eaten a couple of peyote buttons having embarked on a journey in search of their spirit animal, then blamed blacks and Jews for America's diminishing prominence in the world.

I was in the Netherlands for a red-light-district-themed comedy special for Showtime. There were a few Americans on the bill along with several international acts. One of the interesting things about doing comedy in other parts of the world is finding out what translates and what doesn't, and why. I had a joke that involved a reference to swimming pools. This bit consistently gets laughs in the States, but it died in the Netherlands because so few people have personal swimming pools, given the weather.

Also, the Dutch tend to appreciate comedy in a less audible way. They don't applaud after jokes as easily as they do in the States. I don't mind this. I often enjoy comedy without laughing loudly myself. I like the idea of an audience being able to enjoy themselves in subtler ways. Subtle appreciation can allow for more space to communicate because there is less expectation for a punch line. At least that was my experience in the clubs. At the television taping, they laughed more audibly and applauded more regularly, but that's because they were peer pressured by the warm-up act, goading them into making noise.

Television tends to have this effect on audiences in general. Applause becomes part of the culture. If you've watched late-night television and wondered why in the hell these people are clapping for something that would barely get a nod out of a real audience, this is why. They've been told that something special is happening, that what they are about to hear is funny. They applaud out of deference or courtesy. They applaud for the same reason you smile or fake a laugh at a dinner party—because it seems like the thing to do.

After having eaten too many mushrooms the night before, I awoke feeling like I looked—disheveled and hazy. I sat in my little room, gazing through my window. I watched ducks compete for food in a canal and thought about the competition for resources on this planet, the struggle for life. I thought about my father's death. I laughed inwardly at the idea that if my father owned the canal I was looking at, he'd try to find a way to charge the ducks rent. I found humor in imagining the ducks trying to understand the concept of rent. I felt the ache of having lost my father too young. He was too young to die, and I was too young to lose him. I remembered my father in the hospital bed. Tears welled in the corners of his eyes. He looked at me and said, "I don't want to die." He was on a morphine drip because of the pain. He would drift in and out, lucid, then not. He looked out through his hospital window at some men working on the roof of a nearby building. He watched intently for a few moments as they moved about doing whatever people that work on roofs do. Ever the hustler, he turned to me and said, "Look at those snakes on the roof. They're up to something, and I want in." One time, hopped up on morphine, staring at a fish tank, he turned to me and said, "I think the cat tried to fuck one of the fish." His hallucinations were always entertaining.

Sometimes he seemed unable to recognize me. He looked at me as though we may have met at some point. Like he was supposed to know me, but couldn't put his finger on why or from where. But he didn't try to hide it. He eyed me in the same way that he did the rest of the world, suspiciously. I didn't take any offense. He loved me plenty when he knew me.

I was still in my room in Amsterdam. Still looking at canal ducks patrolling their patch of water in search of food. I felt a little heavyhearted, but warm and not all that bad. I looked around at the ancient waterways and centuries-old structures and thought about how I love Europe. I thought about how challenging life in the sixteenth century must have been. I felt fortunate to be here in the twenty-first century. Five hundred years ago, you were lucky if you'd traveled ninety miles from your place of birth over a lifetime, let alone the six thousand I'd crossed to get here from LA. I felt guilty that my father had never managed to make it here. I felt guilty for experiencing so many things that he hadn't. I wondered what it must have been like for my father, growing up without guidance in an environment with so little warmth and so much struggle, an environment where aggression and paranoia were tools for survival.

He died of AIDS. Well, no one really dies of AIDS, but from complications brought about by having AIDS. Though I'm not sure I fully understand the term, I guess he was bisexual. I never knew him that way, but my mother said that he was always interested in men sexually. She also said that she'd known from the beginning of their relationship and it didn't bother her. If you're thinking *WTF*, I'm right there with you.

My mother rebelled against having grown up as a WASP. She found their conventions and institutions hypocritical and disappointing. She didn't distinguish between dinner forks and salad forks; she'd rather eat with her hands. She said that she had accompanied him on more than one occasion to meet up with a male friend of his, someone he had sex with. She wasn't involved, but she wasn't offended by his involvement either. She would just wait outside sometimes. There was a lovely lake nearby, she told me, and she would sit there. I could think of better ways to enjoy nature.

I always found my father's sexuality so incongruous with his personality and his position in life. He was an alpha kind of guy in many ways. He led men in a junkyard. He was the boss of the blue collar, men from tough places who had rough lives, and he was respected by these men. Listlessly, watching the ducks in the canal, I think about how to make sense of it all. I can't. Such is life.

35

ROME
THIS TOO SHALL PASS

I had a week before I needed to be on a plane home. Jessica had agreed to meet me in Amsterdam. She was my girlfriend. She was my friend and my enemy, and my love. The day after she arrived, we decided to take the train to Rome. From there, we were supposed to meet up with several friends of mine in the South of France. We thought the train ride would be romantic, but it wasn't. We argued the whole time.

After arriving in Rome, I haggled my way into a taxi and off we went. What happened soon after this would initiate the most intense amount of travel in a short period of time I've ever experienced or ever hope to experience. In medieval times the Rota Fortunae, or Wheel of Fortune, referred to the capricious nature of fate. Well, she'd turned against me . . . or maybe not.

We arrived at the B&B I had booked. It was housed

in a very old, nondescript—but not without utilitarian beauty—apartment building on a block just wide enough for a horse and carriage to squeeze through. The night was cool, calm, and clear. We waited outside for longer than we should have had to because the night attendant had to walk over from another building to check us in. I called the guy well in advance, but time for Italians is relative. In the States, there'd be no wait, but there probably wouldn't be much to look at either. I didn't mind waiting. It would be hard for me to compliment a city's beauty in a more all-encompassing way than to say, "I didn't mind waiting." I was enchanted. One hundred feet from our door was a river, on the other side of which stood a thousand-year-old castle. The castle was connected to our side of the river by a bridge lined with sculptures—of what, I couldn't make out, but I know they had wings. Café umbrellas hovered over chairs on cobblestone streets all around us. The night attendant arrived, keys in hand. He spoke little English but had a big smile. We hiked up time-worn marble stairs to our room, which was quaint, even lovely in the ways that old, well-built but basic things can be. We dropped our bags and headed back out for a walk. The antique shops were closed, but I could see through their windows: classic paintings amid furniture from bygone eras and hand-painted pottery lit by ambient streetlight. The sounds of motorbikes and leather-soled footware, worn by guys who spend a little too much time worrying about their shoes, echoed through alleys. The cafés began closing. Flowers poured from wooden boxes, floating below wooden shutters, anchored by five-hundred-year-old bricks. It was after midnight, but the odd gelato shop was still awake. For a moment I watched a couple of Italians arguing about something or other. Their hands moved with each word or phrase, like a conductor leading an orchestra after a fight with his wife. I was starving, so I bought a slice of pizza and split it with Jess. The pizza wasn't good or bad. We sat down at an outdoor café. Its walls were lined with ivy. We ordered two glasses of red wine—"Something strong, a cabernet or something," I said, not knowing anything about wine. We waited for twenty minutes for wine that never came. Prompt isn't really their thing. The waiter smiled at me, even though I gestured with my hands and shoulders so as to say, *What the hell takes you people so long?* The wine finally arrived. We were tired, and my knee bothered me a little, so we wandered back for some sleep. Very few experiences live up to the fantasy of what you imagine. Strolling through the streets of this little neighborhood at midnight was better than I could've imagined.

I was happy to be somewhere that had nothing to do with comedy. This felt like an actual vacation. I hadn't been anywhere unrelated to a gig in years. Our second day in Rome was spent walking. We strolled through a marketplace near a fountain surrounded by vendors selling fresh fruit and vegetables. I happened upon a scooter rental outfit and couldn't resist. Jess and

I put on a couple of goofy helmets and hit the streets. Driving through Rome is the opposite of California. You don't wait for people to cross the street. You carve a line in or around them. You dart in and out of traffic as the opportunity presents itself. Outside of the odd red light, there isn't a whole lot of waiting. This was all very comfortable for me. A thing of beauty, really. It's the way I prefer to move through life: at speed, get in where you fit in.

On the advice of my friend's parents, we had lunch at Costanza. It's a little restaurant built into a cave under the ruins of Teatro di Pompeo. We jumped back on the scooter and headed to St. Peter's Basilica, the largest cathedral in the world. It was glorious and hideous. The basilica represents the pinnacle of what humankind can achieve if motivated by inspiration and passion, but it's also a testament to hypocrisy and delusion. Whether or not you believe in Jesus, there is nothing about the garish, ostentatious beauty of a Catholic cathedral that has anything to do with the selfless simplicity and humanity that Jesus represents. Versace couture is conservative when compared with the gold-laden outfits of the clergy's upper levels. When it comes to work clothes, cardinals and drag queens have more in common with each other than either one of them would be comfortable admitting.

On the morning of our third day in Rome, we jumped up, swallowed a couple of espressos, and hit the scooter. Jess kept mumbling about how she was born to ride, how she loved the rhythm of the kill-or-be-killed traffic, so I pulled onto a peaceful side street and let her take the helm. I hopped on the back, put my arms around her waist, and off we went. Jessica's confidence rose with each passing block until we reached a turn. We were about to make a right as several other vehicles pulled up and around us. The light turned green. Jess spazzed, hitting the throttle and the brake simultaneously. I tried to keep us upright by extending my right leg and decreasing the throttle. There wasn't enough time. Accidents are bad enough without having to watch as they happen, and sure enough, down we went. Lying in the street, I felt angry at Jess. I collected myself through the searing pain and hopped back on the scooter to move it from the roadway. Jess was a bit banged up, but nothing too serious. She had bruises, the beginnings of a black eye. We made it back to the B&B, but I couldn't walk. We jumped in a taxi. "Hospital, please."

The wait in the emergency room was no longer than it would have been in any city in the States, about two hours. They wheeled me into the x-ray room. Shortly afterward, I received the bad news. The weight and velocity of the scooter combined with that of our bodies and the position of my leg during the fall had broken my ankle. The doctor told me that I'd need surgery. He said it wasn't that bad, but it wasn't that good; I'd need a couple of screws. They had no open beds at the hospital, and he didn't know when they'd be able to operate.

"Could be a week," he said.

So I headed back to the States for surgery.

On the first leg of my journey back, I began reading a book written by a Buddhist monk. There wasn't much in it that I hadn't heard before, but it was filled with wisdom nonetheless. It had heart. I was going to have to cancel a couple of gigs while I convalesced. I'd have to cancel an appearance at the Just for Laughs comedy festival in Montreal.

The monk said, "This too shall pass." It didn't feel like it then.

I've got a lot to learn about stillness, I thought. The flight home was tough, physically and psychologically. I hoped I'd find an opportunity in it all, maybe find a way to get to know myself a little better. I hadn't had to sit still in a long time. I even fantasized about learning to meditate. I wasn't sure where I'd be staying when I got home, as I'd rented out my place in Venice Beach for the month.

Jess felt guilty, and she was really helpful; she promised to care for me over the next several weeks. She woke up with me in the middle of the night more than once and helped me into the bathroom. She felt bad. I felt bad. I had a standard shift car, so I wasn't going to be able to drive.

I hadn't wanted to leave Rome. The night before we left, rain fell. I could hear the pitter-patter of water on

hard, flat surfaces echo throughout the courtyard below our open window. If I was forced to choose a fa-
vorite sound, it would probably be rain. I wanted to
cry. I held it back at first but told myself that the more
evolved choice would be to let it go. I couldn't remember the last time I cried. So I did—I cried, not just
about this but about my shitty relationship and about
my bad luck. I cried about everything and nothing,
and this.

I was afraid of being in a cast. I wasn't afraid of
surgery or pain. I've always feared being stationary.
Not being able to move around freaks me out, but part
of me also felt a little excited. I was going to have to
challenge myself to find a way to sit still, to not move.
I wanted to figure out more about what makes a lack of
movement so frightening for me. I hoped my broken
ankle would provide some sort of forced rehab for my
mind, or at least a mirror. Either way, I thought, for
better or worse, this too shall pass.

Wheeling through the airport in Rome had been
comical. Between Jessica's bruises and my cast, we must've
looked like the hapless couple in a bad romantic comedy. Like I said, this was the first actual vacation I'd
taken in many years, so the irony of it ending after two
days was a bit much to bear, not to mention the flights
I'd already paid for from Rome to Biarritz, France. I
was sad about not being able to meet up with my friends
in the South of France. I was sad about how little the
people in the airport were being paid to push me around

in a wheelchair after being so kind to me. So many people are doing the best they can and probably feeling like it's not good enough.

Back in the States, Jess drove me to an emergency room. After x-rays, the doctor said my ankle was broken, but she didn't know if I'd need surgery. She said there'd be no way to tell for sure until I saw the orthopedist, but that wouldn't be for a couple of days. We left the hospital and stopped at some Thai place for lunch. It was located in a strip mall. I glanced out the window, which looked directly onto another strip mall. *It ain't Rome*, I thought. I pulled out my cell and tapped the email icon. A friend of mine had emailed me, letting me know that he was now in the South of France. He hadn't planned on going but found a way to do so and was going to surprise me. I read the email to Jess. She said, "Is there any way we can go back?"

"That's ridiculous," I said.

An hour and a half later, we were back at the airport on our way to France.

My friend picked us up at the airport in Biarritz, a picturesque little beach town on the Bay of Biscay in the South of France. It's a little too manicured for my taste, but it was beautiful nonetheless. Napoleon or his wife or someone had built a palace there in the 1800s. I stretched my leg out in the car and felt some pain in my ankle. The airport, now behind us, dissolved in the distance. I looked at Jess. She was happy to be here, and so was I. I still didn't know whether I'd need surgery, but I'd rather not know there than sitting in a strip mall in LA. I rolled down my window and hung my arm out. The warm metal of the door against the inside of my arm felt good. The fresh air in my face felt even better.

We pulled up the driveway and parked in front of the beach house where we'd be staying. Finally, after four days spent in airports and emergency rooms, I was here. I swallowed a Vicodin, grabbed my crutches, and hobbled out behind the house. After nearly falling twice, I sat down in the grass above the beach and leveled my eyes against the horizon. I felt grateful, then unlucky, then grateful again. It could be better. It could be worse. *Thank God I don't have a gig tonight*, I thought. I lay back and felt the earth against my shoulders.

I wondered what the ducks back in that canal in Amsterdam were doing at that moment and whether they'd prefer the weather here. I wondered if the joke containing the swimming pool reference that didn't work with the Dutch would've worked here. I thought about my father and how he'd never been to the South of France. He didn't belong here. Neither did I. I don't feel like I belong anywhere, but maybe that's okay. I'm a comedian. I'm not really supposed to belong.

What is belonging? Comfortable isn't in the cards for me. It never has been, and it never will be. *Maybe that's too fatalistic*, I thought. Comfortable isn't really in the cards for anybody. Maybe the expectation of comfort creates a lot of discomfort. We all feel the anxiety of unanswered questions and decisions we've made or haven't. I wish my father were here. I wish my ankle weren't broken. I wish my relationship were stable, but it isn't. I wish my career were less contingent upon things outside of my control. I thought about the monk who wrote the book I was reading. He probably knew more about my questions than I did. He'd come up against himself and his loneliness without an audience or a microphone. He did so sitting still, looking inward. I don't know if he's found peace, or if he really knows what peace is. I wondered if the universe was aware of itself, and if it had any questions, and what those questions would sound like. Maybe the universe doesn't know why it's here or even if it's here. Maybe the universe feels the pain of a cosmic broken ankle as it longs for its version of a father long passed. Inhaling air perfumed by the sea, I thought about what the monk said. *This too shall pass.* That's about the only certainty any of us have, I guess. This too shall pass.

36

BRANSON CHRISTIAN VACATION DESTINATION

Jess and I broke up after we returned from Rome. We kept thinking we could work. We couldn't. What the fuck was I doing in Branson, Missouri? Traffic was slow on the main drag through town. It was high tourist season, I was told. I'd just passed a sign advertising Dolly Parton's Dixie Stampede Dinner Attraction, then another for Presleys' Country Jubilee. Another sign wearing a Confederate flag read DIXIE OUTFITTERS SOUTHERN HERITAGE STORE—a replica of the General Lee from television's *The Dukes of Hazzard* was parked out front.

Someone told me that Branson is the number-one Christian vacation destination in America. I wondered if my mother had ever been through this part of the country and what she'd think. Then I thought, *Better if she steers clear of Branson*. This place wasn't for her. If my mother lived here, the townsfolk would find a way to bring back the witch trials. I can deal with Christians as individuals, or Dolly Parton, or the General Lee, but all in the same place? Who was this town built for? It's like Vegas rear-ended Disneyland, and they both ended up crashing through a highway divider into the front yard of a Southern Baptist church.

I wasn't sure why or how I was booked there. Someone must have built a comedy club and said to my agent, "Send me someone," then my agent said, "I've got just the guy"—then that guy couldn't make it, so there I was.

At the show that night, I met a girl. She was pale and skinny and pretty in an Olive Oyl from *Popeye* kind of way. She was too young for me, or I was too old for her, but this relationship wasn't going to last for more than seventy-two hours, as I was leaving on Sunday. She said hi after the show, and we exchanged numbers. The next day, I called and asked her if she'd like to meet up for dinner before Friday's show. She was wild and sweet and lost like a feral cat with a lot of energy and no place to go. She was from St. Louis, but she left home looking for work. She was telemarketing on her way to something else, but she didn't know what. I'm sure she was running from something, but I guess it takes one to know one. She drank like a fish. Not full alcoholic fall-down drunk, but I knew she was on her way to becoming one when she insisted on stopping at a convenience store after the bars closed for another six-pack and a can of Monster Energy. She had the gene, that addictive gene. I'm sure her child-hood was a messy place to grow up in. I hope she's well. She was sweet and fun. She made my life better for a few days. I hope I had the same effect on hers.

Being in Branson caused me to question my choices in life even more than usual. I thought about my first time onstage. I was twenty-one years old when I first tried stand-up comedy. I was working on the floor of the New York Stock Exchange at the time. A friend of mine named Dave had begun doing stand-up and was promoting a little show. He asked me to try it, and I said yes. I still don't quite know why I said yes. *What the hell am I going to say onstage?* I wondered. I remember sitting on the subway to work, trying to wrestle a premise into something that resembled a joke. Anyone is capable of a funny idea, a premise. The difficulty is in trying to mold that idea into something that a roomful of strangers will also find humor in.

My first show took place in the theater portion of a gay bar in the West Village called the Duplex. How this show ended up there, I don't know. It was a small room, maybe thirty seats. I don't know how many stand-up shows took place here, but many a show tune was sung and many a feather boa unfurled and sashayed about this stage. I still remember my outfit. It wasn't quite as flamboyant as a boa, but still striking. I wore a puffy orange vest, black T-shirt, and a gold chain. I looked ridiculous, but in my twenty-one-year-old eyes, the mirror said otherwise.

My material was bad, but not awful for a first timer. I don't remember much of my set. I remember telling a joke about a straight guy going into a nail salon, and during the course of his manicure, he realized that he didn't want his nails painted with clear coat, but rather a color, and by the time the manicurist was finished, he'd realized that he was gay. My set was nothing to write home about, but people seemed to like it, and I liked that they liked it.

A lot of stories about a comic's first time onstage seem to involve fear, but also some addictive quality, often having to do with the attention they received from the crowd. I've heard people say, "I was hooked." I've never felt that way about the attention. I didn't hate the attention, and I wasn't going to argue with anything that made it easier to get laid, but I wasn't in love with the attention. Stand-up comedy was a language that spoke to me. It felt more like a calling, like becoming a missionary, if missionaries were more selfish and stayed out late. People talk about how much fun stand-up is for them. I've had a lot of fun doing comedy, but that's not the overriding motivation for me, which prompts the question, what *is* the overriding motivation? I guess it would have to be reconciliation, maybe a desire for a sense of community, to feel less alone. I've always been after some reconciliation, some way to bridge the past and the present.

I remember waking up in the morning as a child and wondering what the hell I was doing here in this world. Why was I tying my shoes on the way to a bus I didn't want to board, on the way to a school I didn't want to attend? It all seemed absurd. It still does, but at least I'm more comfortable in my own skin now.

Those questions can't really be answered, but the anxiety stings less when you have a community to share it with. A roomful of people laughing at a joke I've written based on my experience of a relationship, or the world, or whatever the subject is helps me feel less isolated. It's almost like a support group or a confessional experience with a group of people who are saying, "Yes, it's all fucked up, so let's at least get a laugh out of it. We're all in this ship of fools together."

37

BRANSON ACTING CLASS

It was around this point that I had decided to join an acting class. I was curious to see what it was all about. I remember watching some movie star and thought, *Seems like a good gig.* I didn't really know what actors did. I was not raised on theater. Hell, I had never even been to a theater. I was curious about it, but highly skeptical.

I signed up for an acting class. My teacher was steeped in a New York theater tradition that approached acting very seriously—"a craft," he called it. I was drawn to the way he spoke about the value of plays, drama, and the exploration of human behavior. He imbued acting with a sustenance and intellect that I had never associated it with.

Still, I didn't fit in. I was used to that feeling, though in this case it wasn't such a bad thing. Not fitting in with an acting class doesn't generally result in fistfights. And unlike a number of the guys I hung around with at the time, I could easily take most of the actors in my class. I felt like a Stallone character trying out for the tennis team.

A couple of months in, I found myself desperately wanting to cry. Half the guys in the room had already cried during a scene, and I felt as though I had to wrench out a couple of tears out of a sense of competition. Crying out of a sense of competition is rarely good for a scene and almost always embarrassing for the fool doing it.

Acting has been described as "living truthfully under imaginary circumstances." I decided to stop emoting out of a sense of competition and tried to serve the truth of the scene. Turned out that was the right choice. I found myself really engaged by a search for the essence of something—authenticity. I walked away from my first few classes with a greater respect for the craft.

I even decided to take a "movement class" after my teacher suggested I do so. The objective of a movement class is to enhance your body's ability to act through a scene—to free you up, to help you become a more sensitive instrument. The logic was, if you were "blocked," then you weren't communicating as effectively as you could be. Our movement teacher was going to show us how to get out of our own way, especially in the context of an emotionally charged scene.

Class was held in a dance studio—old wooden floors and mirrors. I entered the room with twelve other actors. We were greeted by a tall man with bright blue eyes and the posture of a lightning rod. He wore a tight white shirt, black sash, and black tights. That's right, a sash. Slippers adorned his feet. He walked, feet apart, like a dancer or a duck. He stood, backlit, like a messiah. He inhaled with importance and spoke his first few precious words.

"Hello. My name is Rees. I'd like you all to breathe . . . in deep . . . one, two, three, and out . . . one, two, three."

The tone of his voice combined with the seriousness of his approach brought back memories of my mother's commune, the Land, where people would hold hands before lunch and pray by *om*-ing around a salad bowl. I felt like leaving but used that as motivation to stay. *Deal with your discomfort, Dov,* I thought.

I entered my second class wearing tights and a T-shirt. I've never felt so uncomfortable. If anyone I had grown up with had seen me, I would've had to end my own life by committing seppuku like a disgraced samurai.

Rees dimmed the lights and hit play on a CD. The sounds of the rain forest settled upon us.

"Arrange yourselves in a circle," said Rees, without opening his eyes.

We did so.

"If at any point you feel uncomfortable, you can enter the safe zone. The safe zone is the area around our piano in the corner of the room . . . Now feel the energy to your left and to your right."

The only energy I was feeling right then was my own, and it was telling me to make a beeline for the piano, but I resisted. *I've been in street fights, had my jaw broken, and even had cops pull guns on me a couple of times,* I thought. *I'll be damned if I'm going to be the first guy in this room to seek the safe zone.*

"Now I'd like you to begin moving in place. Let your body tell you how. Do not impose an idea on yourself of how to move. Just move. Do a little floppy bear dance. You're a floppy bear hopping through the forest," said Rees.

I looked around hoping some other guy had come to his senses and we'd find in each other the solidarity to leave. I found no one. Quite the opposite—everyone in this room happily began behaving like their version of a floppy bear. I was left with no choice but to continue. I bit down on my cheek and began moving, self-consciously, but moving. I was a floppy bear.

"Okay, everyone, we're going to sit down now," chirped Rees. "The person you are seated next to is now your partner."

I was hoping that I'd landed next to a girl. I hadn't. My eyes met with the bearded gentleman seated to my left. He looked relaxed and happy to be there, which made me that much more uncomfortable.

"Feel your partner's energy. Take them in," whispered Rees.

Oh, great, an opportunity to be "taken in" by a bearded guy, while wearing tights, sitting on the floor of a dance studio.

"Raise one hand in the air, and align it with your partner's hand, but without touching."

What have I gotten myself into? I thought.

"Point your index finger at your partner's heart."

A few long seconds passed as I reluctantly raised my finger and pointed.

"Now I'd like you to align your index finger with your partner's finger, and bring them together. You should be touching one another's finger."

Images of a piano flashed through my mind like slides projected onto a wall by a strobe light. In slow motion, my partner's finger moved in the direction of mine. He was smiling. My jaw clenched as I allowed my finger to make contact with his. He smiled again. My stomach felt like there was a rock in it, but I held steady. A few beats passed.

"Okay, now we're going to do a little finger dance."

"The fuck we are!" said the voice in my head. I leaped in the direction of the piano, but I didn't stop there. I bypassed the safe zone right into an even safer zone, the locker room. I tossed my tights in the locker, jumped into my jeans, and headed for the exit.

I understand that we can all learn from that which makes us uncomfortable, but I decided then that I would have to do so in my own way. No floppy bear, no finger dancing. I'd have to pick up the lessons I would've learned in movement class somewhere else, while wearing jeans.

This didn't frighten me away from acting altogether, though—only from the more ethereal offshoots. I think I learned a lot in acting class. I learned about human behavior and how much of what we say has little to do with how we feel. Truth means reading between the lines, analyzing subtext and physicality. If someone is apologizing to you, but you can't really feel it, perhaps they're not actually apologizing. And if I can't feel what I'm saying, why should I assume that someone else will? How many times have you spent time in a social setting and left having felt even lonelier than before you had arrived? I have a tattoo on my arm that reads, "Do not speak unless it improves on silence." I'm guilty of violating that precept, but I do aspire to it. Deconstructing scenes in acting class helped me understand more about why I was communicating in the first place. If I'm talking, walking, and moving, there needs to be a reason I'm doing so. If I ever said anything without understanding why I was saying it, my teacher would ask me why I was doing that. If I didn't have an answer, it meant that I had more work to do. It meant that I needed to understand more about who I was and what I wanted. I like to think this kind of work can help create a deeper sense of self-awareness.

Before acting class, the men I'd been around had behaved as though vulnerability was something to be ashamed of. Watching the way these guys related to one another made me think that we'd all be better off if we had ready access to our feelings and less shame around feeling them. I'm not saying we should all be looking for excuses to cry, but I'd imagine that a lot of fistfights have been the result of an inability to do so.

That said, a lot of the guys in acting class may have taken it too far. They could use some toughening up. Tears for the sake of tears are no more effective than yelling for the sake of yelling.

An aside: Can we please stop using the word *courage* to describe some actor's choices during a scene? The whole entertainment business is guilty of developing a culture of superfluous language that serves only to reduce the meaning of the words being used. I've heard the word *amazing* used too often to describe things that were at best good. Can't we save the term *courage* for people who run into burning buildings or donate kidneys? I'm not saying your scene partner in class didn't make a ballsy choice; I'm saying that we shouldn't be describing that choice in the same language we use to describe those who throw themselves on a live grenade.

38

BRANSON SWING SCENE

Acting class was also great for meeting girls. I met a pretty, petite midwestern gal with big eyes and a beautiful voice. She was the ingenue of a Broadway play. I remember the first time I saw her perform. Thousands of people, young and old, sat, rapt, as she sang. Later that night, I mentioned a swing club that a friend of mine had told me about. "Sure," she said. Not swing dancing, mind you—*swingers*, couples that would have sex there or meet other like-minded couples and then head out for more private surroundings. It was housed in an old brownstone, and people lined up outside, dressed in what would barely pass for clothing in any reasonable environment. We were greeted at the door by a guy in shades and a black suit.

Really? Shades? I thought, as if this environment weren't shady enough.

After I paid the entry fee, the cashier pointed me in the direction of the buffet. I didn't eat much, but I tried the ziti—wasn't bad. We ascended the stairs to find thirty or forty people in various states. Bodies were twisting this way and that; some were having sex, some weren't. Others sat and talked, glancing about occasionally. The group operation isn't my scene, so we banged in the bathroom.

Aside from a few dates and whatever I learned about acting and human nature, I made two good friends in acting class. One of them was named Dmitri. He moved to Brooklyn from Odessa as a young Jewish kid. Dmitri began selling heroin by the time he was sixteen. By the time he was twenty, he had purchased a house in cash. By the time he was twenty-three, he had become a junkie. By the time he was twenty-four, he was doing a three-year bid in prison, having lost his house and all his money.

I don't remember how Dmitri found his way into an acting class, but I remember his preparatory routine prior to performing an emotional scene. While most of us would patch together some sense-memory scenario involving a long-lost loved one or a family member who'd passed away, Dmitri would lock himself in a closet and pretend the warrant squad was about to kick down his door.

My other good friend was Jason. He would become my best friend before disappearing for seven years. He hailed from immigrant stock but looked like the captain of an Ivy League athletic squad—which, in fact, he was. He went on to graduate with honors and was the captain of his championship-winning lacrosse team. He was the guy every mother hoped her daughter would marry.

Like other perfect pictures, he wasn't necessarily what met the eye. He was thoughtful, sensitive, and very bright, but he had a dark side. When I say he disappeared from my life for seven years, that's exactly what I mean. One day he was there; the next, he wasn't. He didn't phone. He didn't write. The few friends we had in common hadn't heard from him either. Till this day, I don't really understand what he was going through or why he felt the need to leave. Maybe his own understanding of it is limited. Seven years after the last time I spoke with him, I received an email apologizing for the disappearance and expressing an interest in reconnecting, which I was more than happy to do. Jason did a lot for me. He provided me a window into a world I had never known. When I was growing up, I didn't know any educated people outside of my mother, let alone someone with Jason's résumé. And my mother wasn't representative of any societal ideal like Jason was. My mother lived on the fringes. She didn't have much respect for traditional institutions, educational or otherwise. I was always curious about how the other side lived. For me, Jason represented this side.

I can remember being ten years old at a lawyer's office with my father and looking up at a wall where two framed degrees had been hung. The lawyer was wearing a shirt and tie. His hands were manicured. He seemed clean, excessively so. I didn't know what to make of him. My father, meanwhile, was wearing jeans. When you tow cars, you need to bend down to secure the vehicle with metal hooks, so the jeans had dirt or grease on the knees. My father spoke with his hands and with a manner of speech that seemed to go with the grease on his jeans. He seemed out of place within the gentility of this environment.

I've always felt like the guy in the greasy jeans. And I'm okay with that now. It's part of who I am, though it's taken me a while to earn that comfort. The junkyard had no bookshelves, but there was much to be learned there. And just because the attorney's office had leather-bound books, it didn't mean people really read them or understood them. It didn't mean they knew any more about what mattered than my father did.

Jason more than anyone was the one to help me see that the difference between these two environments could be superficial. Having a wall of books doesn't make you smart. Greasy jeans don't make you stupid. The guy behind the oak desk and the guy under the hood of the car aren't necessarily that different, and if they are, it's not because of the way they're dressed. Part of the reason I understand this is because Jason was my friend. Jason let me know that my thoughts had value, and because he felt that way, I started to feel that way. He told me that I was smart—as smart if not smarter than many of the people he went to school with. Eventually, I began to believe him.

So there I was in Branson, Missouri, the largest Christian vacation destination in America. I didn't belong there any more than the swing club or movement class. I don't belong anywhere, and yet I do. I belong everywhere and nowhere.

39

SOMEWHERE IN TENNESSEE SUNBAKED, DUSTY, AND WILD-EYED

I'm in a white van, sailing down a dirt road. On either side of the road are trees. In between the trees are tents. As the trees thin and the fields begin, I can see large wooden structures used for staging bands. These structures look out of place, like erector sets in a room with no furniture. Eighty thousand people descend on this piece of land every year for the purpose of music, drugs, and fellowship. There are people everywhere, drifting in hives from one stage to another. Swarms of the sunbaked, dusty, and wild-eyed, all looking for something to hear and feel. Someone excitedly tells me that Sting is playing tonight. I like Sting, but I'd sooner jump out of this van and hike back to the hotel with no shoes on than wait on a half-mile-long line to watch him. But I feel that way about all live events.

I'm here at the Bonnaroo Music and Arts Festival

in Tennessee to do comedy. I was told that one of my shows would take place during the day. This is a problem. Stand-up comedy, like vampires, should never emerge into the light of day. It's just not right, like having a children's party at a strip club. The show was to be held in an air-conditioned tent with two thousand chairs. It's ninety degrees outside. I'm sure the attendees, who wait an hour or two on line, are at least as motivated to enter the tent for the AC as they are for the comedy. You could stand up here with a puppet and a blindfold, telling knock-knock jokes, and it'd still be a full room given the heat outside.

The gig goes better than expected. I enjoy walking around the festival in the knowledge that I'd be leaving in another van that same night. I guess I can understand the appeal of a big festival. You feel like you're a part of a village built for people like you. There are no authority figures to speak of; no one to advise you against the consumption of LSD for lunch. No one to say, "Hey, if you smoke that, you may not feel so good, or you may feel too good and begin to believe that you can fly."

Whatever. I'm getting paid to do stand-up. It could be worse. It has been worse. I used to work the worst rooms in New York City. Most of us do in the beginning. You take stage time wherever you can get it—coffee shops, open mics—wherever there's a show, wherever anyone will listen.

Some of those rooms were worse than others. This

is really saying something; the competition for "worst room" is fierce. There are many terrible places to perform, so describing one of them as "the most terrible" is like singling out a pig in a field of muddy pigs as particularly muddy.

40

TENNESSEE
THE PIG

And such a pig exists. Let's call it Comedy Club X. This is the club where I used to compete for stage time in what was basically a showroom in a hallway. Rarely was my name announced much before one in the morning, and when it was, it no longer resembled my name. This was the Puerto Rican show, the one where I had to change my last name to Dominguez once a week for seven minutes of stage time. This place was the single worst—the *capo di tutt'i capi*, boss of bosses—pig among pigs.

Comedy Club X was a black hole, devouring anything and everything in its path, including light and self-esteem. It was in one of the few parts of Manhattan devoid of charm—or at least that's what it felt like to me whenever I was within ten blocks of the place. The cockroaches in the sound equipment deserved better equipment to occupy. The walls were made of cracked plaster and shattered hope. It was comedy's version of a haunted house, except this place could be genuinely frightening.

Every good haunted house needs a crypt keeper. Call him a manager, if you will. In this case, the crypt keeper was a sexually aggressive gay man in his fifties— very aggressive, like a rattlesnake, but more playful. He'd sexually harass anyone and everyone, male or female; it didn't really matter to him. To harass was his passion and his hobby. It was his art form. Anyone can catcall someone from across the street, but the crypt keeper would get up close and personal, looking his subject in the eye when he worked his magic. He would sexually harass with such wanton abandon that most of us couldn't help but laugh. One instance of harassment is terrible, but ten of them, over the course of an hour—among comedians, no less—and things just get funny.

The owner was a bit more sinister. He wore shiny jackets and smoked cigars, as all sinister types should— this way, you can see and smell them coming. He was the embodiment of dishonesty, but the way he dressed let you know what you needed to know, so in a way he was honest; like Pacino's line in *Scarface*, "I tell the truth even when I lie." He would trade stage time for anyone willing to fix the plumbing or mule heavy objects up treacherous stairs from a basement that looked like a crime scene. I once heard him answer a caller's question by saying, "The dress code is casual, and we have a light menu." Dress code? You could've walked into this club with no shirt and a pistol, and the only thing the owner would do is remind you about the two-drink minimum. The menu was indeed "light"; you had a choice between potato chips and a different kind of potato chips. The club's house emcee looked like one of the bad guys from *The Lord of the Rings*. To my knowledge, he hadn't killed anyone, but if ruining jokes were punishable by law, he'd be staring at an electric chair.

I loved it here. No one was watching, and I was able to work on my act with a minimum of judgment, if only because the audience's expectations had been dashed by their surroundings. When a club looks the way this one did, you're not expecting George Carlin to walk in; you're just happy if whoever has the microphone speaks English. The level of comedy they required was not what it might be at other places. It's like riding a bicycle that looks as though the wheels are going to fall off; you're just happy when they don't. You may even begrudgingly begin to respect the bicycle for its ability to be ridden in the first place, given its condition. Perhaps the audience looked at the comedians working here with greater empathy, allowing them to suspend judgment. They may have felt the way one tends to feel when entering a dog pound. It's hard to see the helpless and caged without feeling pity. Essentially, this club was a dog pound for comedians—a place where those without shelter or purpose could come in from the rain.

On some level, everyone that worked there was kind of funny. The staff was funny in the way that people can be when they've been overwhelmed by circumstances beyond their control; their eyes permanently rolling toward the heavens in acknowledgment of the inevitable and the absurd. It was a sort of gallows humor, and even the comedians that weren't funny were made funny by their bleak environment. With surroundings this awful, bad jokes were almost befitting, an accoutrement to the dilapidated wheelchair ramp.

Yes, the people there were crazy and unscrupulous, but they knew it. They were exactly what you thought they were: liars, addicts, and lunatics; no one pretended to be otherwise. These people couldn't help but be what they were. They weren't honest because they were principled. They were honest because they didn't have the craft or the competence to pretend. It was like a psychological nudist colony, one where the people weren't naked because they had removed their clothing but because they had never had any clothing in the first place.

Stage time was hard to come by, so I worked there and anywhere that would have me. Like an animal in winter foraging for food, you ate what you could. Twice a year, the Comic Strip on Manhattan's Upper East Side held a lottery in which over two or three hundred tickets would be given to aspiring comics. They stood for hours on a line that extended around the block. That ticket would provide you with the opportunity to return to that club at some point over the next six months for an audition: a few minutes of stage time in front of someone capable of booking you at the club. The objective was to "pass," allowing you to call in your availability on a weekly basis for the privilege of a five-to-seven-minute spot at the end of the night. Maybe one or two out of several hundred actually passed the audition, and it likely hadn't been their first try. My experience of running around Manhattan in search of stage time was bittersweet. It was a grind, but there was something about the hustle and the horror I enjoyed.

I saw a psychologist who told me that I was comfortable in chaos. This sounds about right to me. There is something about chaos and the people that inhabit chaotic, dysfunctional environments that I feel at ease with. Maybe that's part of the reason people get into comedy in the first place—to create order out of chaos. Conflicting ideas can achieve a sort of cosmic order through humor, and through that order we can make a little sense out of ourselves and the world around us.

41

TENNESSEE LARRY

I think the friends I'd made from this period in my life also found comedy through a need to form order out of madness, though one of them was just plain mad. His name was Larry. Larry was a brilliant comedian, mime, and mimic. His mind worked like a computer chip, processing information at higher speeds than a human being should be able to. He could riff on a range of subjects with accompanying characters, like Robin Williams, but more sinister—think Williams in black leather with a cigarette hanging out of his mouth and dark-circled eyes. He would contort his face and voice in ways that made each character real, and whole, and distinct from the others. At some point, the characters would even begin conversing with one another, giving Larry the appearance of a man possessed.

Unfortunately, Larry didn't just look crazy. Sustaining

a friendship with him required a capacity for chaos that even I didn't possess.

One time, a friend of mine lent Larry money, a categorically bad move if you wanted your money back. I'd lent Larry a few bucks over the years, but I knew I'd never see it again. I didn't mind. I found him so interesting and entertaining, I chalked it up to the price of admission. My friend did not. He called Larry repeatedly, asking for his money back time and time again. Larry finally returned the call and said that he was now flush with cash; he would be happy to repay the loan. That afternoon, Larry showed up at my friend's building and rang the buzzer, saying, "I've got your money; come on down and get it." My friend descended four flights of stairs and met Larry on the sidewalk. He shook Larry's hand, said hello, and thanked him for coming. Larry said, "Of course," then opened a duffel bag that contained some paperwork, a wig, and a half-eaten sandwich, but no money.

Exasperated, Larry turned to my friend and said, "I have no idea what happened."

I don't know what happened either, and I'm not sure that Larry knows or ever will know. It's not important for me to find out or for my friend to get his money back. Larry made the lives of those he came into contact with better, if not a touch more difficult at times. My life was more interesting for having known him, and I'd imagine that's the case for most of the people who called Larry their friend. Some of us aren't meant to be understood, maybe even by ourselves.

Larry was a genius, but you'll never see him on TV. He's not the kind of genius that'll be able to show up at meetings and convince an executive or an agent that he can hold it together long enough to make it to the next meeting. He couldn't be depended upon to harness himself in a way that would permit others to profit from him. I wish there were a place for the lost and lonely, for the misunderstood: the crazy angels like Larry, who on balance bring more into this world than they take from it.

42

TENNESSEE
THE COMEDY CELLAR

My biggest goal when I was making my bones as a comedian in Manhattan was to break into the Comedy Cellar. This was referred to as "passing." The Comedy Cellar is hallowed ground. It is just what its name suggests—a basement situated on MacDougal Street below a restaurant called the Olive Tree Café in Greenwich Village; it's a neighborhood where Woody Allen, Richard Pryor, Jimi Hendrix, and Bob Dylan all came to ply their trade.

The cellar and the café are connected through an interior stairway. The place has history and character and that thing you feel when you walk into a room that isn't just a room. There are beautiful paintings and drawings on the walls of the café. The bricks in that basement, like hundred-year-old sponges, have absorbed far more than their fair share of comedy, angst, stupidity, and brilliance. So many comedy clubs feel like fast-food franchises; too many McLaughs, not enough soul food.

In the back of the Olive Tree Café was "the comics' table," the table where we comedians would sit, argue, listen, and laugh, waiting to descend the staircase that led to the cellar.

The Cellar doesn't feel like it was just built to sell drinks. Manny Dworman started the business. He was an intellect and a musician. He was funny and curious, and he would hold court at the comics' table, reminding comedians what intelligence actually looked like. After Manny died, his son, Noam, took over, and he's as interesting, creative, and intelligent as his father. Estee runs the club, books the acts, and keeps everyone in line, effectively making her the grande dame of live comedy in New York. Manny's wife, Ava, is a wonderful artist, and her paintings adorn the walls of the café upstairs. Charlie Chaplin movies run on a loop until closing time at four in the morning. City life pours through the windows from the sidewalk as slow-moving cars and passersby make their way up and down the street.

The Cellar has class. It's comedy's version of a seventeenth-century French salon, and for me it meant *show business*, or at least the only part of the business that mattered. I don't know if I've ever really wanted anything more than to be a part of that table. It was there that as a lifelong outsider, for the first time, I felt that I belonged. I wasn't there because I had to be or because it was the least uncomfortable place for me but because it made sense to me.

If only the world were more like that table; a place where people can argue in peace, and curse, and question, and love, and hate, and be what they are—as long as what they are is really them. The table will tell you if you're pretending. The table will let you feel miserable and maybe provide some solace or just enough ridicule to make you forget why you were miserable in the first place. The table will be what your family wasn't, and what they were. We're all animals looking for refuge, surrounded by other fragile animals doing the same. The table can offer you a moment's solace.

Or maybe the table will say, "Shut up with your juvenile, existential musings. There is an audience downstairs with their own fears and families and broken hearts. Get over yourself. Go downstairs into the cellar and be part of the people. Go down into the cellar and make laughs. The animals have gathered, and they couldn't care less about your state of mind. So go down into the cellar and tell them something honest and heartfelt. Tell a joke that comes from the thing that unites us all, a joke that reminds us we're all in it together. Go down into the cellar, for we are all animals looking for the sustenance to make it through another winter, and laughter will help us brave the cold until we feel safe enough to emerge."

43

VENICE, CA GATORADE

It's 6:00 A.M., and I've just taken a pill and a half of hydrocodone. The pain woke me up thirty minutes ago, and I can't get back to sleep. I had ACL surgery yesterday. Jessica, the ankle breaker, is lying next to me. She shouldn't be here, but I feel weak-miss-her-lonely, and I could use the help. She says she's been attending individual and group therapy. She's been coming to terms with her childhood. I've always loved her.

It didn't last. A couple of weeks into seeing each other again, things seemed as chaotic as they'd ever been. We broke up again. I knew this would happen. Logic truly is a limited tool. It's as though logic is a lackey for the subconscious; follows it around, opening doors and smiling, but without respect or remuneration. Logic is the subconscious's bitch.

LOGIC: Hey, Dov, Jess has serious psychological is-sues that couldn't possibly have gone away over the last couple of months, so we really shouldn't be get-ting involved again.

SUBCONSCIOUS: I know, but we make love and laugh at least once a day, even when things are bad; combined with the fact that I feel disconnected and lonely.

LOGIC: Well, whose fault is that? You haven't made a concerted effort to move on, let alone engage with others. At least not to the degree that the combina-tion of good sex and a laugh won't plunge you back into the cauldron of a hopeless love affair.

SUBCONSCIOUS: I just had fuckin' ACL surgery, you militant prick. Sorry, I know you're trying to help. Look, maybe I'm rationalizing my involvement by using the excuse that I'm basically immobile and in need of nursing and no-condom sex.

LOGIC: Correct, you're putting our emotional well-being and the potential to learn from an adult rela-tionship at stake because . . .

SUBCONSCIOUS: Is that red wine over there? Dim the lights. Jess is wearing tights. Relax. Is lying to yourself really that bad? Ooh, that's a nice red . . . cabernet?

LOGIC: But—

SUBCONSCIOUS: Shut up, bitch.

The last time Jess and I broke up, it was over a bottle of Gatorade. No kidding. The sun was shining. We were walking hand in hand along Venice Beach when thirst drove me into a convenience store. I pulled the bottle out of the fridge and placed it on the counter in front of the cashier. Jess grabbed the bottle and took a swig, unbeknownst to me, as I was surveying what seemed to be a larger-than-normal selection of gum. The cashier grabbed my attention by saying, "That'll be two bucks." As I pulled out a couple of singles, I noticed that a quarter of the Gatorade was missing. Horrified, because I hadn't seen J drink any of it, I addressed the cashier.

"Someone drank some of this."

"My God," said the cashier, "go grab another one. Sorry about that."

Weird, I thought.

J watched this exchange take place and said nothing. I walked back to the fridge, grabbed an unmolested Gatorade, paid for it, and we left.

Once outside, J turned to me and said, "I drank that."

"What? Why didn't you say anything?"

"You saw me."

"I didn't see you. Had I seen you, I wouldn't have gone back for another Gatorade."

"The cashier saw me."

"No, she didn't."

"Yes, she did."

"What the fuck are you talking about?"

"One of you saw me."

"Are you out of your mind? According to you, both

of us—me and the cashier—saw you, which would've required one of the world's most unlikely conspiracies."

"I don't know what happened," Jess said.

"Well, I know what didn't happen. Me and the deli clerk didn't call one another and plan a self-defeating Gatorade swap with the objective that you and I would then leave the store with another opportunity to argue about something that makes no sense whatsoever."

Jess doesn't experience confrontation as a potential route to resolution. She understands logically that it can lead to resolution, but she avoids it at all costs. This leads to slightly insane incidents like the one involving the Gatorade. It felt like she discovered new issues on a monthly basis. She recently found out that she is easily startled, a condition known as hyperekplexia. I couldn't help but laugh at this one. She'll jump and shake at the sound of a car horn or anything moving at speeds in excess of a tortoise.

"Why are you still in and out of this relationship, Dov?" you ask. Well, I think the answer is a layered one. Yes, there's sex, laughter, chemistry, love, loneliness. And that'll keep you going long after you should've gotten out. There's also the idea that your partner has been working on herself diligently in therapy and genuinely wants to change, and I believe in second chances, and maybe even thirds depending on the context. It should also be noted that she has the tenacity of a mongoose chewing its own leg off to escape from a trap. She wants to get back to where we started. I can't help but respect her tenacity. She's also one of the best-looking people in the world. How the hell am I supposed to resist? I guess it's my fault. If I was healthier, I might be able to stay away. Clearly, I'm half the problem. Who's crazier? The person I think is crazy, or me, the person I think is sane but is still in love with crazy?

44

VENICE, CA
VULNERABILITY

For many, comedy is a defense against vulnerability. Comedy can heal, but it can also lead us astray and prevent us from inhabiting the parts of ourselves that need exploring. I had an epiphany on the evening following surgery: I have major issues with vulnerability. Not to say that many don't, but an issue's relevance is proportionate to the degree that your life is being negatively affected by it. There are those that eat a bit too much sugar, and there are those that swallow whole cakes. I think my issues with vulnerability are of the latter variety—that is to say they are serious and profound and will deeply affect me in negative ways if I'm not able to wrap my head around them.

The day I returned from ACL surgery, I found myself unable to ask for the help I might need. I couldn't ask Jess, as we were not on good terms, and my pride wasn't something I was strong enough to swallow. The doctor told me that I wouldn't be released into a taxi post-op, as it was an insurance liability for them and a health liability for me. I was close to immobile and really needed help making it home from the hospital. I have a few close friends in LA, but I couldn't call them. Why? Not quite sure. This was a clear sign that part of me was broken. I was able to give but not receive.

My close friend Bryan had someone he worked with around his house, a handyman of sorts. I decided to ask Bryan if I could contact his handyman, who I'd pay for a ride back from the hospital. Luckily for me, Bryan refused and insisted that I allow his wife, Amanda, to pick me up, as he was going to be out of town. Thank God. I didn't know it then, but I was going to need help putting my pants on post-surgery, and shudder to think that I would have had to ask the handyman to help out with that. Amanda was wonderful. I was grateful, but being grateful made me uncomfortable as well. It made me very uncomfortable. I had always been the kind of kid that when asked by a friend's parent if I was hungry, I'd immediately respond with a no even if the real answer was yes.

Amanda drove me home from surgery, helped me into my place, and said goodbye. I sat, staring at the wall, feeling lonely and vulnerable as the effects of the anesthesia wore off. But the painkillers were kicking in, and I also felt a bit social, which only served to exacerbate the underlying loneliness. I decided to hobble next door to visit my neighbors, David and Michelle. I've always been friendly with them, and I wanted to see if they were home. Their lights were on, but their shades were drawn. I've never knocked at their door unannounced when their shades were drawn, but this was a different story. I was post-op and a little high. I hobbled in a circle in front of their door for about a minute and a half, procrastinating, at which point I decided to make my move. I knocked twice, but softly. David opened the door and looked at me and my heavily bandaged leg, my crutches. His warm smile said, *Come on in, you poor bastard.* The look on Michelle's face said the same. I moved through the door like a dog that had been caught peeing on the carpet. I felt shame for having knocked. I couldn't admit that I wanted to see if they'd be around for the next couple of days in case I needed something, in case something went wrong. I guess I also wanted to say hi to a friend, to feel like I wasn't totally alone.

David and Michelle asked if I was okay and if I needed anything, and I thought, *Oh, right, I knocked on your door, and now I'm just standing here.* Instead of being honest and vulnerable and just saying that I was there because I wanted to see if they were going to be around, but also because I was feeling isolated, I found myself making up a story. I lied. I told them that I was expecting a package in a day or two and that I might need some help with it. I followed the first lie up with another. I said that I'd be making some granola and wanted to know if they'd like some. I could barely move, let alone produce granola, an observation that I'm sure wasn't lost on them either. Under the best of circumstances, I'm not confident in my ability to produce quality granola, let alone gift it to my neighbors. These are not the actions of a balanced person.

I'm continuously surprised at how deeply affected we are by defense mechanisms we developed as kids. My issues with vulnerability and debt have everything to do with my father, and the junkyard, and subsequently, my choice to do stand-up comedy.

For my father, accepting help meant that you now owed the person that helped you. To owe someone isn't necessarily a bad thing. Sometimes it can be an opportunity for closeness that you wouldn't have had otherwise. Owing gives both parties an opportunity to get to know each other for better and for worse. For my father, however, to owe was only bad. In the world he came up in, with the father that he had, in the junkyard that he lived in, owing meant a lack of defense. My father could do for others but didn't want anyone to return the favor. He would not owe. He would not be vulnerable.

Like my father, I couldn't accept help, let alone ask for it. I wouldn't owe. In stand-up, you perform and then you leave, but you don't owe, and you are only vulnerable insofar as your material is honest and heartfelt. But you set the limits, and you aren't any more vulnerable than you allow yourself to be.

Stand-up can be a way of expressing your value to

the world when you feel valueless. You're saying, "Here, look what I can do. I can entertain you." But when the entertainment ends, you're left with yourself: alone, unentertained. Doing a show isn't really reciprocal. You need them, but they haven't necessarily affected you in a meaningful way. My energy is directed outward. There is plenty of energy being returned from the audience, but that is hard for me to feel. I can't do enough for those around me, but I also can't owe.

I must change this. Without being able to owe, I can't truly receive. Receiving means that you hear the applause and the thank-yous, and that you owe grace and gratitude in return. After doing a set, sometimes I feel as if I've given something that helps maintain my distance from others. I'm protecting myself from something when I longer need to. I am removing myself from the kind of debt that would enrich my life, by allowing for the kind of closeness that can only come through that same vulnerability.

LOGIC: We need to find meaning.

SUBCONSCIOUS: No problem, just don't accept any gifts.

LOGIC: Gifts? You mean don't ask for help?

SUBCONSCIOUS: Start asking, before you know it, you owe.

LOGIC: Without the ability to owe, we don't learn as much about ourselves. We build walls and live behind them, which isn't really living.

SUBCONSCIOUS: Did you make that granola?

LOGIC: Can't I just thank my neighbors for being there for me and provide the same for them, without paying them off, which is really a way to buy myself out of owing; buy myself out of that kind of scary closeness.

SUBCONSCIOUS: We should pick up oats on the way home.

LOGIC: I'm not making granola.

SUBCONSCIOUS: Shut up, bitch.

45

ALASKA
COLD, PURPLE NIGHT

Alaska was beautiful, and the mountains were majestic and foreboding. On the way to the gig, I drove down a stretch of highway called the Turnagain Arm Drive, a ribbon of asphalt outside of Anchorage. To my left were mountains, and to my right was what looked to be a bay but with very little water. It was low tide, and it looked as though the sea had left but promised to return. There were pockets of water in vast pools, like shiny oblong coins without faces. Beyond this were more mountains, and beyond them was the ocean. I was on my way to Anchorage for a gig. Apparently, there's a guy who promotes a show and flies in comedians a couple of times a year. It's not a great gig, but I wanted to see Alaska, so I said yes.

Anchorage isn't charming. It's cold and utilitarian. It feels more like a big town than a city, and not in a good way. There are tourist shops selling stuff meant to look like it was made by indigenous people. One of the shops has a sign out front that reads Real Eskimo Crafts. It's hard to imagine that the Inuit worked much in pink nylon, so I'm thinking a lot of this junk was made in Mexico or China. It feels both wrong and inevitable, commodification. Proud people made their lives here before this shop began selling salmon jerky, plastic canoe key chains, and stuffed animals.

I stood on the sidewalk before the show and looked up. It was cold and clear. It was a postcard: the moon over the mountain line was big, and the sky was purple and dotted with stars, like thousands of mini chrome rims suspended in the atmosphere. The way that postcards are meant to evoke emotions, this place made me want to believe that this part of the country is populated only by those that can appreciate it: nature-loving frontiersmen, maybe a few scientists, the odd recluse.

But the truth is that not everyone is here by choice. Some of them would rather be anywhere else. But there's work here, mostly in fishing and oil. I hope whoever came here for the money can also see and feel the majesty of the mountains. Looking up filled me with that "small, in a good way" feeling. I was at one with my euphoric smallness. I didn't want to go do a show. I felt the need to apologize to the atmosphere. "Hey, gotta run. I have to entertain intoxicated strangers in a beer hall. Goodbye, endless night and the closest

I've ever felt to the idea of a benevolent creator. Hello, dick jokes."

I wondered if the stars had a sense of humor. It's hard to imagine a star laughing, but what's laughter if not a strange energy brought about by circumstances we don't really understand? If words and sounds can elicit laughter, then perhaps the universe is a humorous one, and if so, why can't the stars, and the red giants, and the black holes be in on the joke?

The saloon where the show was held was filled with working people who seemed to want their jokes loud, fast, and dirty. Their attention wasn't easy to get, but once it was gotten, they were cool. They calmed down and reduced their chatter to the point where I was able to pretend that having this show in this room wasn't such a terrible idea after all. The ceiling was way too high, and the light didn't focus attention in the direction of the stage the way a performer hopes it would. The gold rush theme, wall-mounted animal heads, and pinball machines didn't exactly say *cutting-edge comedy*, but I made the choice to enjoy it.

Einstein said, "The most important decision we make is whether we believe we live in a friendly or hostile universe." I guess he meant that the choice will become a self-fulfilling prophecy. Kind of like positive thinking, but in a way that I can relate to—not that *The Secret* bullshit about visualizing a Mercedes. If you choose to believe the universe is friendly and surrender to some kind of energy (quantum or otherwise) in the form of your own openness, then perhaps it will feel and become friendly. If we choose to believe that we are separate from and not part of the fabric of the universe, then we'll need to fortify ourselves against a cold, uncaring, and ultimately painful reality. We're born, we live, and we die. I'm going to choose to believe that the universe is friendly even in the face of so much evidence to the contrary.

46

LOS ANGELES
THE TONIGHT SHOW

Which brings us back to Hollywood. Years ago when I first landed in Los Angeles for meetings, I was trotted out in front of a number of network executives charged with the job of finding talent. They were development executives, essentially talent scouts for television shows. It's their job to meet with writers and performers in an attempt to determine how or if they can be utilized. The central question was, can we plug this person into a network show or develop a show around said "piece of talent"? They seemed more interested in me before I told them that I wanted to do a show about a guy who had just been thrown out of school for punching his professor in the face during an argument over solipsism, the belief that nothing exists outside of your own consciousness. In their defense, I didn't know how to pitch a show or take a meeting. I had just performed in a comedy festival and was seen by an agent who liked me and set up a bunch of meetings on my behalf. After this, I ended up doing some stand-up on television. I did something on Comedy Central and then one of the after-midnight night talk shows. The year after that, I submitted a DVD to *The Tonight Show* and was given the go-ahead. I sat in my dressing room before the show and looked at my reflection in the mirror for a moment. Jay Leno stopped in to say hi. We talked about stand-up and life on the road. He seemed like a nice guy, or at least he was nice to me, which is what people really mean when they say so-and-so was a nice guy. After a couple of minutes, Jay left to do his job, and soon after, I did the same.

To walk out in front of a studio audience, knowing I only had four and a half minutes to make an impression—I felt it in my stomach. Standing behind the curtain, Jay announced my name, and the producer gave me the thumbs-up. I walked into the bright lights and did my thing. The audience liked me, and so did Jay. The show tapes in the afternoon, so I was out of the studio by 5:00 or 6:00 P.M. The sun was shining, but something about the natural light felt dim as I emerged from the studio, back into normal life. It wasn't that I didn't want to return to life. It's that I wanted to come down more gently; from an atmosphere charged with the energy of a "first time" back to the mundane wasn't what I'd imagined. I wasn't looking for fanfare, but something, anything, to distinguish this moment. I wanted someone to say, "Hey, great job. Wanna come hang out with us and celebrate a bit?" It wasn't to be. The producers had a job to do, and Jay probably just wanted to get home and wax one of his cars or something. It's LA; you do what you always do: walk into a parking lot, get into a car, and steer onto a highway. *Be careful of expectations*, I thought. I remember when I got my first and only studio movie. I was still living in New York at the time, and my agent called me about an audition for a film called *Invincible*. It was based on a true story about Vince Papale, a thirty-year-old bartender from South Philly who ends up trying out for the Philadelphia Eagles and making the team. Mark Wahlberg would play Vince, but the rest of the cast hadn't been determined yet. I hadn't had much professional acting experience, but I'd done a cool indie film, a few national TV commercials, and some really bad off-off-off-Broadway stage plays. I showed up at the casting office and read for the part. The next day, they called me back to come in and read for the director and the producers. I got the part. Next thing you know, I'm living in Philly for three months and shooting a movie.

I really enjoyed it. I love creative energy and being part of a team. I love good movies and people that give a care about their work. That said, there's the hype and the reality. The reality of acting in film is "hurry up and wait." You're going to be spending a lot of time in your trailer, waiting for a knock at the door.

Knock—time to go to makeup.

Knock—time to go to wardrobe.

Knock—time to go to set (this knock doesn't come enough).

I'm not complaining. I was happy to get the job. Whenever people ask me about the movie or working with Mark, they have a look on their face that says, *How great was it?* It was great, and annoying, and the hours were both short and long, and I'd love to do it again.

People often ask me whether I prefer stand-up or acting. They aren't incomparable, but sometimes it feels like they are. I have to write the stand-up. As an actor, I have a script. I memorize lines, work on the scene, develop the character, and show up in the morning. Stand-up requires a different skill set. You don't stay in one location and work with a collective. You don't collectively do anything. You write it alone. You perform it alone. You go back to your hotel room alone. It can be tough, but when it's right, and it's personal, and it comes together, nothing really compares. You're living in a moment that you've created. As an actor, you can shoot the scene again—and you will, many times. You are surrounded by a team of people that act like they care even if they don't. When push comes to shove, I prefer to live or die in the moment. The energy of immediacy is a tough one to put down. It's pure stuff. It hasn't been stepped on, and that can be addictive. In the moment, live, under lights that can feel hot even when they aren't, you have to do the thing. You've got one shot. That's all they'll give you. You can't stop and say, "That didn't feel right." You're not on a set that is closed and controlled. As a stand-up, if something doesn't feel right, you swallow it and keep moving because no one cares and no one will help you. You're on your own, for better and for worse.

After *Invincible*, I was hired to play a cop on an NBC detective series called *Raines*, starring Jeff Goldblum. We were on the air for half a season before we were canceled. The ratings and the reviews were okay, but we were on the fence. NBC hired a new head, and he gave us the ax. No hard feelings. This is what we signed up for. The new guy always wants to put his stamp on programming. His résumé and potential legacy will have much to do with what shows were developed under his watch at the network. Our show wasn't doing badly, but it wasn't a hit, and if you're on the fence, and the new guy isn't in love with you, say goodbye. Entering the entertainment business means that you'll be looking for a job for the rest of your life. This isn't necessarily a bad thing. It beats many other lines of work, and it may be the only one for me, but it's always a roll of the dice. In TV, there's no way of knowing if the job will last a month or a decade.

In the end, I just want to work. I want to do good work that feels like I'm fighting the good fight whether or not the war is futile. I want to be of service. I want to feel alive, and if that takes place on a set or on a stage, or writing in a room by myself, that's what I'll have to do. I can appreciate Alaska, but I can't live there. In some ways I wish I could. I envy the recluse's self-reliance but not his solitude. I like the idea of living off the land and controlling my own destiny on my own little patch of earth without feeling so dependent on the mercurial business of show or other people, but I hate fishing. Manual labor has never been my strong suit, so I wouldn't be much of an asset in the oil fields. I'd probably end up telling my boss the truth—that if Satan wanted to run a company, an oil company might be on his short list. So would a movie studio, come to think of it, though for different reasons. Maybe that would be for the best; Satan would be too busy making bad blockbusters and banging actresses to damage the climate and endanger wildlife.

47

LAS VEGAS
BACK AT THE BEGINNING:
KIND OF

I'm seated in the back of a purple, mid-nineties limo, looking up at long, thin, rapidly pulsating neon disco strips attached to black velvet roof liner. I'm on the way from the airport to the casino hotel where I'll be headlining a small New Year's Eve show. I'm glad the "Vegas-fixer-guy" who works for the entertainment director insisted that I not take a taxi, availing me the opportunity to wait an extra thirty minutes for the privilege of a lift—ten minutes from the hotel—in this atrocity. The driver is a real character. Back at the airport, he introduced himself as Rick. Rick has blond feathered hair and a shiny green button-down tucked into pants so tight I can't help but wonder if he's late for his real job at a male strip club or as a coke dealer in the late seventies. It's as if someone bought this limo contingent upon the salesman's sweetening the deal by throwing in a driver designed by the very person who built the car. My face wrinkles a bit out of curiosity.

"Nice rig," I say, thick with sarcasm.

Rick, dead serious, shoots me a wink in agreement, as if I am a woman complimenting his physique. I like Rick, but nowhere near as much as Rick likes Rick.

Uniquely alone, as one tends to feel in the back of an eight-passenger vehicle without seven other people, I pull a magazine out of my carry-on and begin reading an article about a wealthy man who walked away from his career on Wall Street in an attempt to find himself and to fill gaps in his scientific and philosophical knowledge. For a moment, I wonder how he'd feel if he found himself in the back of this limo. Would he be horrified? Would he laugh in the presence of absurdity? Would he wonder what unforeseen events could have culminated in this moment, in this car, in this desert? Did he feel like I feel right now before he decided to leave Wall Street in search of a more examined life?

Maybe he's here now. Maybe the protagonist in the article is actually Rick the limo driver, and he's conducting some kind of sociological experiment in an attempt to understand more about human nature, and consequently about himself. What drives the questions? Why do we need to know who we are? It's been said that the unexamined life is not worth living, but why not? I'm sure our planet would feel like a more reasonable place to live if people spent more time examining themselves, but are there any lives really not worth living? What makes an examined life worth more? Is *my* life worth living?

I don't really have a choice but to examine. While I was growing up, my life made little sense to me—my parents, my name, the world of the junkyard, the fact that other kids didn't like me, the fact that girls started to like me, the notion that I was funny. They all occurred in a way that defied explanation. Decades later, things still don't really make sense.

I walk into my hotel room and flop on the bed. Ah, Vegas. Staring up at the ceiling, I notice part of the Sheetrock looks like it's been repainted. There's white bleeding into a different shade of white. It's subtle, but noticeable, like a Rothko. *If Rothko had been a painting contractor, he'd have been fired*, I think. I imagine Rothko with outstretched hands, trying to communicate his position. "But, boss, can't you see I was going for something more emotionally evocative?"

My eyes drift across the room and land on the alarm clock. The show starts in under an hour. Thank God. I want out of my head. Fuck all this introspection. I get up and lay out my clothes: black leather jacket, jeans, and boots. I walk past the mirror on the way to the shower and think about how my body isn't as good as it used to be. I feel a little shame, then more shame for the vanity. I suit up and dab a little cologne on each wrist before rubbing it onto my neck. The rhythm of the cologne application reminds me of when I was a kid in Jersey, getting ready to go out for the night.

I grab my little red notebook off the nightstand and head out into the hallway. The carpet under my shoes is soft. I hop into the elevator and land at the lobby. Sounds from the casino flood the opening elevator doors like water rushing into a submarine with a crack in it. It sounds like action. I like action. I walk past a tableful of poker players and think about how they like action too. This thought worries me. I don't want to think right now. *Shut up*, I tell myself. As I round the corner, I can see the last of the line heading into the showroom. They've already dimmed the lights, which means the emcee will be kicking things off any moment now. I get to the bar and nod *What's up?* to the bartender, and he nods back. I order a Stoli on the rocks and take a sip. The bartender lets me know it's on the house, but I leave a ten anyway. This way he knows I'll take care of him, and if I need anything else I won't have to wait too long. I pull a pen out of my pocket and write something on my hand to remind me of a couple of new bits I want to work on.

After about twenty minutes, I make my way backstage, knowing I'll be up soon. I say, "What's up?" to the showroom manager and take a seat against a brick wall behind the curtain. Hearing the emcee say, "Please give it up for . . . ," I get off my chair and look for the little break in the curtains, which leads to the stage. I have trouble finding it, causing me to bumble my entrance a bit. I use it to get a laugh.

The show starts well. The crowd is in good spirits tonight. Table talk is at a minimum, and they're focused and laughing. I notice two girls near the stage looking at me the same way I looked at them. They're drinking heavily and checking their cell phones. They're in their midtwenties. They laugh at the less nuanced parts of my act and seem a bit lost when I begin talking about something subtler. They're enjoying themselves, but for them this show is most likely a way to kill time before they hit whatever nightclub they're dressed for. You don't wear heels like that in Vegas to call it a night too long before the sun comes up.

The old argument returns—the voices of the be-spectacled, analytic angel of my CONSCIOUSNESS and the devil of SEX, DRUGS, AND DISTRACTION. Again, I'm including alcohol in my definition of drugs. Also, for purposes of clarity and tone, I still have no problem with sex, drugs, or alcohol, unless they become a "problem."

SEX, DRUGS, AND DISTRACTION: I love this job.
CONSCIOUSNESS: What is that supposed to mean?
SEX, DRUGS, AND DISTRACTION: It means exactly what I said.
CONSCIOUSNESS: Nothing means exactly what you say.
SEX, DRUGS, AND DISTRACTION: Shut up.
CONSCIOUSNESS: We'd be dead by now if I did that.

SEX, DRUGS, AND DISTRACTION: You see these two broads in the front row?

CONSCIOUSNESS: *Broads*, really? Yes, I see them. Is that what you mean by "I love this job"? Because you know what this behavior leads to!

SEX, DRUGS, AND DISTRACTION: A threesome?

CONSCIOUSNESS: A potential threesome for tonight, intense loneliness and a hangover for tomorrow, and more self-medicating behavior that will only serve to distance us from the sense of self we're searching for. Columbus didn't find the New World by drinking vodka in a disco.

SEX, DRUGS, AND DISTRACTION: Columbus was a murderer, and it's a nightclub, not a fuckin' disco, you square.

CONSCIOUSNESS: Columbus was the wrong example, however—

SEX, DRUGS, AND DISTRACTION: However nothing. I'll deal with you tomorrow. It's New Year 's Eve, and we're going to have a good time!

CONSCIOUSNESS: Stop furnishing your dysfunctional version of reality by describing your behavior as a "good time." It inhibits us from developing into the kind of person capable of attracting the kind of woman who could be potentially fulfilling and sustainable, maybe even challenging—the kind of woman who may actually alleviate some of your whiny loneliness.

SEX, DRUGS, AND DISTRACTION: You're right.

CONSCIOUSNESS: I am?

SEX, DRUGS, AND DISTRACTION: Yes, but it's New Year's Eve. I wouldn't respect myself if I listened to you.

CONSCIOUSNESS: You *don't* respect yourself.

SEX, DRUGS, AND DISTRACTION: Well, you respect yourself too much. You're trying too hard.

CONSCIOUSNESS: I'm compensating for you, dummy.

SEX, DRUGS, AND DISTRACTION: Gotta close the show now. We can talk later.

CONSCIOUSNESS: We won't get to talk. You're going to end up at a nightclub with these two girls.

No, I'm not.

The show ends with a flourish of applause. The people enjoyed themselves. I head back to the bar and order a drink. A couple in their late sixties comes up to me and thanks me for a good show. I wonder what brought them here, and I like that they came. I thank them for their kind words, but do so with my head down, a little embarrassed about some of the subject matter in my act. They didn't seem to mind. I shake hands with a few more people as they walk by and say nice things. The high-heeled, cell-phone-checking girls appear out of nowhere. One of them said, "Good show, I'm Clarissa," and the other one introduced herself as Chloe.

CHLOE: Whatcha up to?

ME: I don't know yet.

CLARISSA: We're headed to some club, supposed to be poppin'. What's the name of that place, Chloe?
CHLOE: Liquid or Fire or something.

Awkward pause.

CHLOE: You drinkin'?
CLARISSA: You should hit this spot with us. It's gonna be poppin'.

Clarissa did a little two-step after she said the word *poppin'* again, and Chloe joined in.

CHLOE: We gotta head out. Come on; we're on the list. Gotta table too.
CLARISSA: You look good for an older guy. Well, not older, but older than us.

I would have asked them to go out somewhere if they hadn't already asked me. Chloe orders three shots, and I tell her I don't like shots, but she jams a heel into the floor, says, "Come on!" and I give in. I ask the bartender when he gets off and let him know where we're headed if he feels like meeting up with us. He looks at Clarissa and Chloe and shoots me a wink that says, *Lucky guy.* Clarissa checks her cell phone again as we head in the direction of Liquid or Fire.

Back on the casino floor on the way to the club, right behind the poker tables, I see someone that looks familiar. *Is it—? Nah, what are the chances?*

It is.

It's the prostitute with the angel wings tattooed on her back. The one I woke up with the last time I was in Vegas. The one from the beginning of this book. I look directly at her, and she looks back. She smiles at me, but right before I say hi with a wave, I realize that she doesn't remember me. She smiles the kind of smile that wants to sell you something, not one that says, *I know you.*

CHLOE: What are you looking at?
ME: I thought I saw someone I knew.

I wonder whether the girl with the angel wings was able to stick to her New Year's resolution to be more healthy by cutting down on sugar. I laugh out loud at the ridiculousness of it.

Then, in a flash of self-awareness, I think, *At least she made a resolution. I can't remember the last time I did.* This stops me in my tracks. Clarissa and Chloe stop too.

ME: Sorry, I appreciate the invite. I'd like to come, but I can't.
CLARISSA: You okay?
CHLOE: It's gonna be poppin'.
ME: I can't.

A brief pause occurs before Clarissa looks at Chloe. They both shrug. Clarissa says something that sounds like "Okay," and Chloe says, "Good show," and then they're gone. I'll be replaced in minutes.

I think about what Einstein said—"The most important decision we make is whether we believe we live in a friendly or hostile universe"—and I want to believe that we live in a friendly one, but in order to honor that decision, I have to earn it. It's an active decision, not a passive one. I have to examine my life. To not do so would be to not honor what I am, to not be what I am. I can't go to Liquid or Fire tonight. I can't spend the night numbing myself with alcohol and the company of people I don't know. I can't go to Liquid or Fire tonight. I have to earn my decision. I *want* to believe in a friendly universe.

Walking back to my room, I think about my father and the life he lived—little in the way of happiness, all the while providing me with any talent that I have been lucky enough to receive. I owe him. I owe his memory. I owe my mother. I owe the junkyard I grew up in. I owe my brother. I owe my friends. I owe Toothless Frank, Deaf George, and Black Lou. I owe Big Mike, my grandfather, and the thieves. I owe Walter from my basement. I owe my mother's commune. I owe the kid who told me about skinny leather ties. I owe the guy who introduced my father to crack. I owe MacDougal Street and the Comedy Cellar. Maybe I even owe myself.

Opening the door to my room, I reach for the light switch, but then I don't turn it on. I don't really need it. The Las Vegas Strip is obscenely bright at night. There is enough ambient light to make out the little desk, beyond which are the plate glass windows. If the only thing separating you from the sky is glass, is that a window or a wall?

It's painfully quiet right now. I pull the pen out of my pocket, along with the little red notebook it's attached to. Opening it, I can barely see the page, but when I put pen to paper, I can make out the words. I write, "resolution . . . write . . . write yourself into being." Then, scrawling individual letters into formation:

Fuck, I hate myself.

I take a deep breath and realize that what was true a year ago feels a little less true today. Little latent fireworks intermittently pop on the other side of the window/wall. Putting pen to paper, I continue:

Cigarette butts and mini-bottles from the mini-bar keep company with cocaine residue on the coffee table.

Hemingway was right about Paris being a "moveable feast," but he failed to mention that so is the rest of the world. I will write myself into being.

48

BROOKLYN
CRISIS OF CONSCIENCE

When is a book finished? I'm not sure. The last chapter you read had been written two years ago. That was the end, or at least it was supposed to be. I began this book searching for myself. What am I? Where am I? Where do I want to be? How do I find meaning? How do I orient myself in such a way that meaning is even recognizable?

Two years ago, I put down this manuscript and didn't pick it back up until I was prompted to do so by my agent. I had a crisis of conscience. I had decided to leave Los Angeles and head back to New York after my last breakup with J. I sold my place in Venice and moved to Brooklyn. LA was never home. Every time I walked into a comedy club in LA, I heard someone talking about Twitter or Instagram. I get it. Social media is here to stay. Sometimes it felt like people cared more about how many followers saw what they had to post and less about what they were saying. I felt like I wasn't saying much either. I'd go out on auditions and show up for spots at comedy clubs. I became more involved in the real estate business. I wasn't inspired, to say the least.

I blame myself for this as much as I blame the entertainment business. Sure, the parts I was auditioning for weren't generally inspiring. But so what? If we're waiting on someone or somewhere else to inspire us, we may be waiting on a train that isn't coming. I was the perpetrator and the victim of my own lack of inspiration. I have to be disciplined enough to find inspiration. I have to hunt, not wait for it. I can't assume it'll tap me on the shoulder. I didn't get into the entertainment business to do business. I wanted to reconcile my life, and sure, getting laid and having fun was a draw as well. But mostly, I wanted to feel like I was connected to something more meaningful and expressive, something that helped me feel more alive. If it was just about money, I could've stayed on Wall Street or spent more time and energy pursuing real estate deals.

I needed to go find stuff to say. I needed to find things to care about. I feel kind of ridiculous and self-indulgent saying all of this. The things I'm saying are clearly "white guy with enough to eat" problems, but if I want to increase meaning in my life, then I have to address them nonetheless. I knew I'd have to pay an opportunity cost for leaving LA, as the television and film business are more prevalent there. I was willing to pay that price. It's not like my career was on fire there anyhow; I don't want to make it seem like I was walking away from some big, potentially glorious project out of quiet dignity. I'm not that dignified, but I like to think I have some integrity, and I really am chasing peace of mind. New York certainly isn't handing that out on the corner, but I'd be more likely to find some of it there. I knew myself well enough to know that. It's not that I wouldn't live on the West Coast for the right job. It's that I want to live in a place that doesn't require that I have the "right job" in order to feel comfortable living there.

That being said, I didn't want to write anything, let alone continue working on this book. I hate sitting. I was supposed to edit what I had written and turn the manuscript in to my publisher, but without a deadline, I didn't. I couldn't find the wherewithal. Sitting down to edit what I had written felt torturous. God, I hate sitting. I couldn't stand my own voice.

As an artist, I felt like a fraud and a failure, and maybe I am, but that doesn't mean I have to stay that way. Did I really want to act or was I more interested in being famous—always a recipe for disaster? I want to be a great stand-up, but what does that mean, and what's the price I have to pay to get there? Am I talented enough? I believe I am. I believe in my talent, but how much of it is talent, and how much of it is something else? I have to focus my mind. Should I cut my losses? When I hear people obsessing over their social media presence, I feel a bit nauseous. Does that mean I have integrity, or does it mean that I don't care about fame enough?

Almost three years after I began writing this book, I'm moving. I'm creating meaning. I did what I said I'd do. I left LA. I'm reconciling. I've finished this damn book. I shot my second one-hour comedy special, and I'm back out on the road, working on my third. I've begun working more as an actor, booking roles in Judd Apatow's *Crashing* on HBO and playing an Internal Affairs detective in *Shades of Blue* on NBC with Jennifer Lopez and Ray Liotta. I just finished shooting a sizzle reel with a great producer for a pitch we developed using real people from my life. I even hired someone to rebuild my website and help me utilize social media. It's hard to think of art as a business, but it is sometimes. And sometimes it's not. It's up to me to be better at both.

I even began talking to J again. We hadn't talked for a year. In the meantime, she got involved in therapy. I started therapy again as well. I saw her as being responsible for a lot of the chaos in my life, but I still loved her. Therapy helped me to see the part I played in the chaos. I wrote J a letter.

Dear Jess,

It's 2:30 a.m. and I'm tired, but I can't sleep. I'm really happy, but I'm sad. I'm nervous.

If someone was to ask why I want to get back with you, why I want to get back with a woman I called crazy and dismissed as someone I couldn't marry . . . Well . . . first I might respond with, "I love her"; I might say, "I love her in a way that I didn't realize I could love her. Not in the way that you love someone over candlelight and a bottle of wine when things are going well; I love her in a way that makes me want to hold her in my arms in the morning while she's still asleep. I love her in a way that almost wants her to catch a cold so I can take care of her at her worst, when she feels unattractive and messy, and emotionally volatile. I love her in a way that makes me want to cry when I think about how I hurt her. I love her in a way that makes me want to tell her I love her even if she doesn't say it to me; even if she doesn't feel it for me. I love her." I didn't understand how much fuel I added to the fire of confusion and abuse in our relationship. I chalked it up to "I lost control, but she's crazy, so that's why I lost control." That's bullshit. The truth is that I'm a bit crazy, and if I were stronger and more secure in my own value, I could've weathered the storm. We may not have worked. We may have broken up, but we would've done so without my behaving in ways I regret; in ways I feel terrible about. Instead of saying, "Jess, you're crazy," I wish I would have been able to say, "I don't understand you, and I'm afraid you're going to break my heart. I saw my mother as having broken my father's heart. I saw him as a bit broken, and I swore I would never break." . . .

When asked why I wanted you back, I might say to this person that I experienced Jess's inability to communicate and engage with me as a dismissal of my very being; as a dismissal of my effort and my love. This really fucked me up. I didn't understand how to ride the wave of confusion and was terrified of being overwhelmed by it. Instead of finding the language to communicate this—language I really didn't have at the time—I lashed out like a fear-biting dog, trying to look fearless but ultimately being consumed with fear. A fear bite is the opposite of strength. If I was confident in my ability to weather the storm of my own emotional well-being and sense of self, I'd bite only when I needed to. I didn't need to bite Jessica. I needed to let her go, but I couldn't. I didn't have the strength.

Looking back from the vantage point of a broken heart and a year in therapy, I realize that she did appreciate me in the way that she could. She was doing what she could. Hell, I was doing what I could, but it wasn't enough. It wasn't even close, but I didn't know it. She showed me love in the way that she could, but I couldn't feel it.

I can now see the part of her that couldn't speak; the part of her that was so noisy on the inside, so frightened of confrontation that she couldn't speak. In the family she grew up in, speaking didn't work. It just made her crazy family crazier, so she learned not to engage, not to validate. When I confronted her, she would ignore me or deny or placate. "Won't happen again," she would say without taking me in or listening.

I used to experience her silence as not caring, not giving a fuck, not being capable of being my partner. I was offended because I didn't know how to hear her. I didn't know how to talk to her. I didn't know how to knock at the door of her heart again after my first knock hadn't been answered. Instead of kicking in the door, I wish I would've sat outside on the ground with my back flat up against the door and waited until she opened it. I wish I had the patience and the sense of self-worth to wait, and when she opened the door, instead of yelling, I wish I could have quietly said, "Please talk to me. Please. I feel really alone, and I've invested so much time and so much of myself in this even though you may not feel that way. I feel nervous because I love you and I don't want to lose you, and I feel like I'm losing you. And if I lose you, I'll lose a part of myself."

I wish I could've told her that she had the power to break my heart and leave me stranded in the emptiness of myself.

> *I'm sorry I hurt you. I didn't know that I was behaving like a fear-biting dog when you needed a companion.*
> *I love you, Jessica,*
> *Dov*

A year after I wrote this, we were married. I don't know how this ride ends, but I want to enjoy it. I want to make it mean something. I want to look out the window and see things in a new way. I don't really know how to do any of it, but I'm closer than I was three years ago.

Things with Jess still get tough from time to time, but we have love and effort. We know ourselves better than we did. We have a fighting chance. Hopefully, we'll learn how to better extinguish the flames while they're still small, before they consume us.

I hope the same for all of you.